ONCE LIFE MATTERS

A New Beginning

Marty Angelo
with Michael Clark

Marty Angelo Ministries
3600 Harbor Blvd. - Box #359
Oxnard, CA 93035

http://www.martyangelo.com
marty@martyangelo.com

Once Life Matters: A New Beginning
Marty Angelo Ministries
3600 Harbor Blvd. - Box #359
Oxnard, CA 93035
Web Site: www.martyangelo.com

ISBN 0-9618954-4-6
Copyright ©2005 by Marty Angelo. All Rights Reserved.
First Edition 2005-Second Printing-06/01/06
Published by Impact Publishing
www.prisonimpact.org
Kalispell, Montana
Coauthor: Michael Clark
Cover design by Gary Carlson
Editor/Proofreader: Kathy Ide

Manufactured in the United States of America

FOREWORD

Every prison has a few hip wise guys like Marty Angelo who write their own rule book and then end up in the dumpster. The difference with Marty is that he is a survivor who learned from his madness. *Once Life Matters* is a rollercoaster ride from the rock superstar spotlight to the prison jungle and then to higher ground.

The '70s Love Generation world of rock stars, drugs, and dropping out crushed many megastars and left the audience staring at its belly button. Marty Angelo survived the front-line madness of that music, drug, and prison world. He came out the other end of the psychedelic tunnel with a fascinating story of out-of-this world freedom.

Marty is an old friend who has been there and done that several times. His story will be a déjà vu experience for many fast Freddies and hot honeys who never wanted the party to end.

Jack "*Murph the Surf*" Murphy
author *Jewels for the Journey* and
minister, Champions for Life Ministries

ENDORSEMENTS

"I've known Marty since I first met him in prison. Shortly after that he came to work for us, and I was able to watch with delight his growth in Christ. From the glittering lights of the music industry to a prison cell and back now to serving the Lord, Marty's story offers hope to all of us. It's a terrific testimony to God's redeeming grace."

Charles W. Colson
founder, Prison Fellowship Ministries

"I have found that as we are being conformed to the image of the firstborn Son, the taker has to die and the giver has to live. Marty Angelo is a giver and I commend his work to you."

Bishop Frank Costantino
author, *Holes in Time* and founder of Christian Prison Ministries and Bridges of America

"More than two million Americans are 'doing time' in jails and prisons. Most of them are doing it the hard way: one dreary day at a time. But some have 'turned their lemons into lemonade' and have redeemed the time by taking Bible study courses and every educational opportunity afforded them to prepare themselves for a different lifestyle than the one that led to their incarceration.

Marty Angelo is one of those men, and *Once Life Matters* is the inspiring testimony of exchanging drugs and alcohol for eternal life in Christ. He gave up his career in the rock and disco music business to become a 'Good News' carrier to the people in jails and prisons. Marty and a small army of ex-cons share a passion to comfort others with the comfort that they have been comforted of the Lord.

For fifty years I have had the privilege of being close friends with these very special evangelists and I have accompanied them in prisons 'where angels fear to tread'. They have read the Good Book that said, 'I was in prison and ye visited me.' (Matthew 25:36)

I was privileged to read the manuscript before it was published and my prayer when I finished it in one night was that it would be placed in the hands of every inmate in America to inspire them to follow Marty's example."

Mickey Evans
founder, Dunklin Memorial Camp

"Marty is a true servant of the Lord. His faithful ministry to the 'least of these' speaks volumes regarding his character. I am pleased to endorse his book and affirm the call of God upon his life to 'go and make disciples.' Your understanding of who God calls and uses to His glory will be expanded in these pages. Take a brief look through Marty's eyes into the future and more specifically into an expanding and ripe harvest field. Get ready for your assignment."

Monty Christensen
author, *70x7 and Beyond* and founder
of Prison Impact Ministries

"After wielding incredible success in America's music industry, Marty Angelo awakened and realized the emptiness in his soul. His resultant conversion to Jesus Christ effected personal transformation in which he discovered real power, prestige, and peace. Now detailed in this life-changing testimony, *Once Life Matters* stands as a must-read for all Christian believers everywhere.

"For more than twenty years, I have walked alongside Marty Angelo, witnessed his life transformation, felt his passion, and observed his committed life as a godly man of sterling Christian character. Indeed, his stature and grand successes in the American music industry pale in comparison to the giant that God molded, shaped, and made. To God be the glory for this glorious testimony and wonderful trophy of God's grace."

Dan Butler
pastor, International
Pentecostal Church, Bellflower,
California

"In my book *Reflections through the Window,* I tell the story of my being a young boy living in the '50s. A teenager in the madness of the '60s and a casualty of the '70s. As with Marty in the '80s God began to put His plan together in our lives.

Together we used our gifts in ministry with Prison Fellowship and have kept in touch these many years. I'm so excited to see his story of how God has worked in his life now in print. I know God will use it to bless many as they search for real freedom."

Ron Sharp
author, *Reflections through the Window* and
Reflections from Within

"Marty Angelo is a humble servant

devoted to Jesus Christ with a passion to share His love."

Mel Goebel
author, *The Unseen Presence* and president of Impact for Life Ministries and Library of Hope

"As Marty's sister, I was there to see God turn his life inside out, and upside down, in a miraculous way! I've shared his story with many people and I've seen the effectiveness of it in people's lives. *Once Life Matters* is gripping and inspirational and I know God will use it to win thousands of souls to Christ."

Joanne Moeller
Marty's sister

ACKNOWLEDGMENTS

Special thank-you to: Our Lord and Savior Jesus Christ, my parents "the late Martin and Marie Angelo," my sister in two ways (Joanne Moeller) and her family, my brother (Louis Angelo) and his family, my daughters (Brigitte Kittel and Michelle Hardie), Bro. Charles Mahaney, Chaplain Warren Schave, Christian Prison Ministries, Coalition of Prison Evangelists (COPE), David and Susan Jackson, Detective Frank Rossi, Faith Farm, Frank and Bunny Costantino, Gary Carlson, George Arnold, Governor Al Quie, Impact for Life Ministries, International Prison Ministry, Jack and Kitten Murphy, Jews for Jesus, Johnny Moffit, Kathy Ide, Mel and Jane Goebel, Michael Clark, Mickey and Laura Mae Evans, Monty and Holly Christensen, Pastor Albert Dillon, Pastor Bob Hoekstra, Pastor Dan Butler, Pastor Gurnade and Bonnie Brown, Pastor Howard Davis, Pastor Luis and Anna Lopez, Pastor Ron Libby, Pastor Tommy Reid, Prison Fellowship Ministries, Prison Impact Ministries, Rico and Vicki Lamberti, Ron Sharp, Rudy and Marie Cegielski, Teen Challenge of Southern California, Temple Aron Kodesh, The Drug Abuse Foundation of Palm Beach County, the LaManto Family, the late Rev. Garland "Pappy" Eastham, and other friends and family.

Once Life Matters: A New Beginning

by Marty Angelo with Michael Clark

Introduction
Why Are We Here?

This is not a Hollywood exposé.
Names have been changed, but not so much
to protect the innocent, as there are few innocent people involved. No, this is the story of
how I went astray and how you can avoid the
mistakes I made. I want to tell you how I
found a whole new life and what I discovered
while finding it. I've faced many problems in
the fifty-plus years of my life, most of them
brought on by myself. I hope you will find
my story helpful. I believe God's purpose for
my life is to tell others what happened to me
so they might find their way back to Him.

My life has been a messy series of
events that combined to create a mosaic—the
way tiles combine to create an image. As sor-
did as some of those experiences were, I
don't have any regrets and I don't look back
in despair. Why? Because they led me to
Jesus Christ and salvation. Many people
never find God, whether their experiences are
good or bad. I want to help people realize

that they have an opportunity right now to be a part of God's kingdom here on earth.

> *Behold, I stand at the door, and knock: if any man hear my voice, and open the door, I will come in to him, and will sup with him, and he with me.*
> **(Revelation 3:20)**

I was always searching for something but was never satisfied when I got it. I searched for the next big music trend, my big show business break, and the next chance to get high. I was always after something. I kept putting things off, hoping for a better future.

> *But seek ye first the kingdom of God.* **(Matthew 6:33)**

Once I learned about my relationship with our Lord and Savior Jesus Christ, and the true meaning of what He does for us, I realized that we could have the peace of God right here, right now. Even when we made mistakes, God was there to forgive.

My story is not so much about what I experienced in my two and a half years in prison and seven years on parole, but my life before and after. The most dramatic time in my life came just before I was sentenced.

2

That's when I found salvation.

> *Therefore if any man be in Christ,*
> *he is a new creature: old things are*
> *passed away; behold, all things are*
> *become new.* **(2 Corinthians 5:17)**

It took me thirty-five years, but I
finally found peace through Jesus Christ. The
decades of the wild life I led, along with the
few times when I was close to finding the
right path, weave an amazing story. I'm not
proud of the many problems I created for
myself—the incredibly stupid things I did—
but I'm not running from them or trying to
cover them up either. In fact, by telling my
story here, I hope you, dear reader, can learn
the lessons I learned without going through
the trials and dangers I faced.

Ultimately, this story isn't about me.
It's about Jesus Christ and how He willingly
and faithfully pulled me out of a lifestyle that
had little hope. I can never repay that love
and faithfulness, but I'm not supposed to.
That's the beauty of grace.

Those of you who already know Him
understand grace. If you have a relationship
with Jesus, you'll find my story interesting to
compare with your own. Then you can share
it with a family member or friend who might
be in need. This could be the spark of

encouragement they need to begin their own relationship with Jesus Christ.

Part of the reason I want to tell my story is to help people understand that no matter how bad things might get you can change and start with a clean slate. You can find Him, just like I did. How did I do it? It's all here. Please read on.

Chapter 1
The Trip Downhill

I woke up in a daze, having just gone to bed at eight o'clock in the morning. I heard noises and looked outside my bedroom window. On the grass in the backyard, I saw at least twenty men crawling on the ground with rifles. A powerboat pulled up next to my roommate's boat.

I'd been staying with a friend on Hibiscus Island in Florida. Usually, when I gazed out the window, all I saw was big cruise ships docking. The view that greeted me now looked like a company of armed soldiers.

"What is going on?" I yelled, though I knew no one else was home.

Concerned that someone was trying to kill me, I picked up the phone and dialed 911.

"Men with guns are surrounding my house," I screamed.

Before the operator could respond,

my bedroom door blew open. I dropped the receiver. Several men stormed my room like an assault force. And they were wearing uniforms! Some were police. Others, federal Drug Enforcement Administration. I even saw some members of the U.S. Coast Guard. A full crime task force.

Two police officers grabbed me, shoved me around, and pulled my hands behind me. They slapped handcuffs on my wrists. As the lock clicked, I realized that I wasn't scared by all the chaos. I was actually relieved.

It's over, I thought. *Someone has finally stopped me. Thank God.*

That thought—"Thank God"—was just a figure of speech, a reflex. I wasn't really thanking my divine Creator for what was going on. I didn't really know God, not then.

The police hauled me down to the Dade County Jail and booked me on various drug-related charges. I'd been in jail before, but this time felt different.

Don't they know who I am? I thought as I sat in my cell. *I'm a big shot in the music business. I don't belong here.*

But sitting there in that cell brought me back to reality.

You're a nobody. The words popped into my head. *A loser. And you always have been.*

I looked back at my life, and I didn't like what I saw. It seemed like a jumble of confusion, aimlessness, and depression. I realized how little I had valued my life. Had *anything* I'd done up to that jail cell moment mattered?

My friends Gus and Chick Driscetti, who rented the house I was staying in, were under suspicion too. We sold just about everything we owned to pay attorneys' fees, including a clothing shop Gus and Chick had. At that time, lawyers' fees for drug cases in Miami were the highest in the country.

Statistics showed that the government caught only 1 percent of the drug dealers in this country. Whoever was unlucky enough to get arrested paid the price for those who got away.

A local lawyer I contacted from jail told me his fee was $250,000 — in cash, up front. "And that doesn't guarantee you'll get off," he said. "A lot of dealers think my fee buys them their freedom. It doesn't. I don't pay off anyone with your money."

I wanted to die.

After a full weekend sitting and stewing in jail, I was dragged before a federal judge for arraignment.

"What kind of work do you do?" the judge asked.

"I'm in the music business, Your

Honor," I said. "I listen to records for a living."

Everyone in the courtroom broke into laughter.

"That sounds like an interesting line of work," the judge shot back. "Just how does one go about getting such a job?"

I briefly explained how I'd reached this point in my music career. The judge seemed impressed. He asked the officers who'd arrested me if they found any evidence to back up what I was telling him.

"Yes, Your Honor," one of them said in an irritated tone. "We found hundreds of record albums and a sophisticated stereo system. But this guy is a drug dealer. He should be kept in jail."

The judge disagreed. He reduced my bail from $500,000 to $125,000.

Before I walked out of the courtroom, the judge told me he had a grandson who wanted to work in the music industry. He asked if I knew someone who would give the young man a job like I had.

"He can have mine," I said.

No Kind of Life

My parents reluctantly put up their house as collateral for a bond and bailed me out. All charges against me were turned over to the grand jury for further investigation.

"Further investigation?" I asked the temporary local attorney a friend retained for me. "How long will that take?"

He told me he wasn't sure, but that it could take almost a year until they got around to it. "Sometimes the grand jury drops the charges," he said. "It all depends on the evidence. So stay out of trouble. The last thing you need is to get arrested again."

"You don't have to worry about me," I assured him. "I don't want to spend another night in Dade County Jail."

After my arrest, my roommate and I were evicted from the Hibiscus Island house. Chick found another place and continued to do the only thing it seemed like he knew how to do: deal drugs.

The trouble we were in didn't seem to matter to him. "We'll beat the case," Chick assured me. "We've got one of the best attorneys in south Florida."

But I couldn't believe Chick. I knew what I'd told a friend on the telephone, the statements I'd made about arranging for him to buy drugs. If the government had a wiretap on my phone line, I was going to be indicted.

Wanting to avoid another arrest, I decided to move in with my new girlfriend, Vivian. She had a nice apartment in Miami and we got along fine.

It was tough going back to a straight line of work after realizing what a fortune could be made selling drugs. Even though I made a decent living in the music business, that was nothing compared to the money that could be made selling drugs. I hadn't been in it long enough to have made *big* money. But after getting arrested, I was afraid to try anything more.

I'd brought all my stereo equipment to Vivian's, and I stayed active listening to records. I tried to contact Eddie Rivera from the International Disco Record Centre, where I had a VIP membership. I wanted to re-establish my relationship with him and his organization. But reality hit hard. Eddie didn't even return my calls.

"I'm finished in this business," I told Vivian.

Two months went by and nothing happened. Then Gus and Chick surprised me one day by telling me I had to find my own attorney.

"Our guy said he thinks it would be best if each of us had a separate attorney," Gus explained.

"I don't have that kind of money," I said, more discouraged than ever.

This is no kind of life, my mind groaned in silent frustration. *Everything I do turns out wrong.* I wished I had some sort of guiding voice, an inner compass to steer my life by. But I didn't know how to find that or if such a thing even existed.

I thought about suicide a lot. Had even tried it once. It had been a horrible experience, one I had no intention of attempting again.

> *There is a way which seemeth right unto a man, but the end thereof are the ways of death.*
> **(Proverbs 14:12)**

"Guess I'll just ride this one out," I told Vivian.

Trouble Keeps Finding Me

News of my arrest traveled fast. All my music business contacts started treating me like I was dead. People I'd thought were my friends deserted me.

"You're too hot," one of my buddies told me. "Everyone is afraid you're going to drag them down with you. It's best if you don't try to contact anyone."

I was thirty-five years old, and "Party Marty" no longer had a party to go to. Sex, drugs, and rock 'n' roll was supposed to be all I could ever want. I'd had plenty of all three. *Then why am I so messed up?*

My sister sent me tracts, books, and

tapes about Jesus Christ. She told me she was praying for me.

"I wish she'd stop praying," I once told my mother. "The sooner the better."

I didn't read any of the books she sent, but I did read the tracts on a few occasions. I also studied the Bible and told myself that if I could ever figure out the book of Revelation and the 666 beast it talked about, I would start paying more attention to God.

I also listened to an audiotape by an evangelist named Hal Lindsey. He'd written a book called *The Late Great Planet Earth* and produced a movie by the same name. I saw the movie while I was stoned on pot. I thought it was pretty cool.

Hal Lindsey seemed to have life all figured out. "This guy makes sense," I told Vivian. "The world is coming to an end, just like he says."

Vivian agreed to listen to the tape with me. Afterward she said, "You're nuts. Maybe you should just pack up your stuff and get out of here."

But I didn't have any other place to go. I had no job, no money, and no prospects.

So, to keep Vivian happy, I threw away my Hal Lindsey tapes and books and played only music on my sound system.

Is This the Bottom?

I took Vivian with me on a trip to California. She liked it so much she decided to stay. She flew back home to Florida without me and started making plans to move to the West Coast. She called me a few days later and told me our relationship was over.

I grabbed the next plane to Miami. But when I got to her apartment, she refused to let me in.

"Don't do this, Vivian," I begged as I pounded on her door. "Don't you know I love you?"

I didn't know if I really loved her or not. But I couldn't handle another rejection.

I opened my suitcase and pulled out a pint of cognac and the bottle of Valium I kept on hand for a heart condition. I swallowed the whole bottle and downed the pills while gulping the cognac and kept pounding on Vivian's door until I passed out.

I woke up the next day in Vivian's parents' house. They told me she'd called them in the middle of the night and they came over and brought me to their place. They had lost a son to suicide and wanted to help me.

"Why don't you call your parents and see if you can go live with them?" Vivian's father suggested.

I wasn't interested in their advice.

All I had left was a white Cadillac, about $100, the clothes on my back, and a trunk full of records and videotapes.

This is it. I've reached bottom.

Or so I thought.

Chapter 2
The Long Road to Nowhere

I didn't really fear death. After all, I was a member of one of the wildest generations ever born in the US. Probably the wildest generation anywhere. Most of us knew death could be right around the corner with the push of a button.

When I came of age, the newspaper headlines told of riots and Vietnam. The Cuban Missile Crisis, The John Kennedy assassination, Bobby Kennedy's killing, followed by Martin Luther King's murder. We lived through Woodstock, the Kent State massacre, and Haight-Ashbury. Peace, love, music, and drugs. What more could anyone want?

But it didn't start out that way. In fact, for most Americans born after World War II, the late 1940s and all of the 1950s were marked by prosperity and good times.

We were "war babies," the Baby

Boomer generation. World War II was the war to end all wars, so bringing up children in a land of peace was assured.

None of us thought we were part of a generation destined to go wild. We looked at life through the rose-colored glasses that were a cultural icon of the times.

But throughout my childhood, I could never understand why I was born. What was my purpose? I wanted to find meaning in life, but couldn't figure out how to do it. I searched in all the wrong places, starting with small steps but taking enough bad turns to stay on the wrong path.

Born in 1946 and raised in a prosperous family, it looked like I had it made. I never went hungry or worried about having a place to sleep. My loving and caring parents provided everything I needed and most of what I wanted. My father was a doctor; my mother, a registered nurse.

I was born in Buffalo, New York. The first house I can remember was on a beautiful street named Humboldt Parkway. It had a big strip of land down the middle of the road, separating the two sides of traffic. That created lots of space for my sister, Joanne, and my brother, Louis, and I to play.

My first loves were soldiers and cowboys. I spent hours by myself, winning battles and pretending I was a famous general. Even at that young age, I often wondered what war was really like. Did people actually die?

Where did they go when they died? My play soldiers never died. Even after losing battles, they were still there.

When I wasn't playing war games, I pretended I was the important sidekick of Roy Rogers, the television cowboy hero of the day. I never missed a show.

Those old programs beamed into our living room in brilliant black and white. Color TVs hadn't been developed yet, but that didn't matter to me. I was still amazed.

Every time the national anthem played on TV, my father rose from his chair, put his hand on his heart, and stood at attention. A loyal veteran, he'd spent most of World War II in charge of a troop hospital train in Europe.

My father and mother—both first-generation Italian-Americans—felt great pride in the fact that their fathers had helped build the railroad around Buffalo.

I had no idea why my father stood at attention in front of the TV set whenever the anthem played. I just figured it must be what everybody's father did.

The Ways We Learn

I had a lot to learn. And I did learn

a great deal as I grew up. My mistake was that I didn't plan. I didn't set any long-term goals or think about the future.

I had good intentions when I was a kid. Though I wasn't exactly filled with a godly outlook, my first real desire was to be a Roman Catholic priest. The same toy chest that was a battlefield for soldiers, cowboys, and Indians became an altar. I draped a bath towel around my neck and over my back as a cape—my priestly vestment. I used a mass missal as a pretend holy book on my altar. One of my parents' wine glasses was a chalice and little pieces of bread were communion hosts. That was about as close to having a purpose in life as I got when I was a kid.

Fantasy and reality weren't that far apart. I attended Roman Catholic schools and became an altar boy. What a proud moment! I looked forward to attending church services and helping the priest. The rest of my friends did the same and we all argued over who got to serve wedding and funeral masses. Weddings, especially, as they were happy occasions, and they always brought big tips.

I held pretend masses almost daily right through third grade. But being an altar boy brought temptation. During mass, I stared at the little wafers the priest blessed, which then became Jesus. *Wouldn't those be better for my mass than plain old bread?* I wondered.

My first opportunity to steal communion wafers came when I was alone in the sanctuary after serving mass. The priest left to take care of some business and I was sitting there, eye to eye with unconsecrated hosts. They hadn't turned into Jesus yet, I rationalized, so who would care? I helped myself to a handful of wafers and ran home to my toy-chest altar. I finally had the missing ingredient to my church service. It never occurred to me that I was stealing. Or sinning.

After that, I took a few wafers whenever I had the chance.

Before long the priest realized that there were never enough hosts for mass. Someone had to be stealing them. He conducted an investigation. One of the other altar boys, whom I had confided in, told the priest that I was the wafer thief.

One day, while I was in the midst of a pretend mass service in my room, my mother led the priest in and they caught me red-handed with one of the stolen wafers. He was very angry and lectured me on how wrong it was to steal. "Especially communion hosts from the church." My punishment was obvious. I was dismissed from altar-boy duties.

I was heartbroken at first. But I soon

took on an attitude that I would use many times throughout the coming years. "Who cares?" *Who needs to be an altar-boy anyway?*

At that point, and for years afterward, the answer increasingly became, "Not me."

The Trouble with Growing Up

When I was eight years old, my father decided to go back to school to become a neurosurgeon. So our family moved to Richmond, Virginia. For me, the distance between Buffalo and Richmond was far greater than the five hundred miles of highway between the two cities.

I still attended Catholic school and church, but with an attitude that continued to grow more defiant. Getting caught stealing communion hosts from our church in Buffalo didn't leave too deep a scar. In fact, the lack of any punishment beyond the loss of altar-boy privileges left me with little respect for authority. *What's the worst that could happen if I did something else?* I'd wonder. If that was all there was, bring it on. The thrill of getting away with something outweighed the risk.

My next challenge was stealing the little milk cartons that were given us by our teachers to collect money for the poor. I didn't need the money, but I stole it anyway.

I only made a few dollars in this theft. I think I knew I would eventually get caught. Even that awareness, though, didn't matter to me. I don't remember now if I was punished when the teachers and principal finally caught on that I had heisted the charity money. I had to pay the money back, that much I remember. But the rest just faded into the void that should be my memories of those days.

Now I can look back on my childhood and see that any problem situation I got into put another dent in me. I might not have suffered direct consequences from my mistakes, but each one hurt my spirit. I covered up these hurts with my party-all-the-time attitude and an outward appearance that said, "I don't care."

It didn't seem that anything in life really mattered.

I wish I'd have known God at that point in my life. I'm sure a relationship with Jesus Christ would have made a big difference for me. I would have cared. But I didn't even know how to go to Him. I had to learn how to seek.

My dad finished his studies in three years, after which we moved back to Buffalo. But Humboldt Parkway had changed. It had turned into a tough neighborhood. The bicycles my dad bought for my brother, Louis, and me were stolen the first night we parked them in the garage.

Catch Me if You Can

Home wasn't home anymore. Because of the problems we found when we moved back to Humboldt Parkway, my parents moved the family to the suburbs in 1957. That was the trend for middle-class families at the time.

We moved to Williamsville, New York, about ten miles from Buffalo. Just before the move, I was exposed to rock 'n' roll music.

Times were changing and so was music. I remember listening to, and liking, Glen Miller. He was the biggest recording star of the day. But then Bill Haley and the Comets started getting some exposure on the radio. Then came Elvis, the Everly Brothers, and Chuck Berry.

Rock 'n' roll appealed to me, to say the least. Somehow, it just fit me. At last, I had found a defining force . . . but still no guiding light.

Most of my friends were heavy into Elvis Presley. They started combing their hair like him and wearing black leather jackets and black pants. As usual, I followed the trend. *We're different*, I thought. *And cool, man, cool*—a favorite expression of the '50s.

My move to Williamsville, New York, brought me face to face with suburban life. *These people are weird,* I thought. The teenagers had short hair and wore little belts on the backs of their pants. The girls wore white socks, saddle shoes, and funny-looking puffy dresses. Everyone was in a clique. Two of the most popular ones were the Trench Coaters and the Rockers.

Making friends came hard for me. I wanted to keep my image of a tough-guy rock 'n' roll type. But the popular soundtrack for the suburbs at that time was the music of Johnny Mathis, a smooth-singing, moody type of guy.

My parents enrolled me in the nearest Catholic grammar school. I wasted my time hanging around the playground with other Elvis-type guys (the Rockers clique) and bothering the boys with the Princeton-style haircuts (the Trench Coaters). It was a natural animosity.

All my classes were taught by nuns, and it didn't take them long to find out that I was not one of the good kids in class. I spent endless hours in detention because I always got caught doing something wrong.

Still managing to put things over on people, I got to be an altar boy again. I guess the priest didn't check with my old church and never found out about my wafer-stealing efforts. I had to have been a sight with my altar-boy outfit and Elvis hair, but I didn't care. I was in it for the same reason every other boy my age did it: because it got me out of class early.

Most of my time was spent serving mass for a priest who held out his chalice an extra-long time while I poured wine from a container. I poured a bit, and the chalice was still there. I poured some more, and the chalice was still there. I poured almost the entire bottle into his cup before he put the chalice to his lips. Then he drank the whole glass. It was only seven o'clock in the morning, and this priest drank all the wine from the container. *If he can do that,* I thought, *why can't I?*

At eleven years old, I stole a full quart of wine from the sanctuary and drank every drop with my friend while we sat in a movie theater. We both got sick. But we didn't think it was so bad that we wouldn't try it again someday soon. Little did I know that this first taste of alcohol would lead to hundreds of future drunks.

My second stint as an altar boy didn't last much longer than the first. My tough-guy attitude kept getting me into trouble in school, so I was fired. *It was a waste of time anyway,* I told myself. *Who needs it?*

Grammar school ended without much fanfare. I was fourteen years old and normal, or so I thought. But I had my share of problems. My parents and teachers forced me into counseling with a priest who consistently told me I would never amount to anything. So when my years at St. Peter and Paul Grammar School ended, I was glad to put it far behind me.

Chapter 3
Life as I Knew It: Numb

I refused to go to the local Catholic high school. I'm sure the teachers and administrators there, no doubt wise to advance word of my reputation, weren't too disappointed.

I enrolled in the Williamsville public school system and began high school. I got involved in sports, especially football and soccer, though I never found athletics very rewarding. I was a fast runner but never wanted to practice. My only thoughts were about girls, music, and drinking.

As I continued to grow up, I noticed myself begin to change. I didn't find much acceptance as a rock 'n' roller. One girl I was beginning to like, Jacky, wasn't into that kind of music. She wore white socks and saddle shoes and was always trying to convince me to get a haircut. I figured if I did, I'd stand a better chance of having Jacky as my girlfriend, so I made the change.

The local barbershop was called Randy and Jeff's. The two guys who owned the shop both specialized in the Princeton haircut, a close-cropped crew cut with a part on the side and all the hair combed over the top of the head. It looked like a military cut with a tiny tuft of hair dangling high on the forehead.

At least I looked respectable. It didn't seem to matter to anyone if I really *was* respectable, as long as I looked the part.

At last, I had found acceptance into the suburban scene. My Buffalo days seemed to be far behind me. I was growing up and would soon be starting high school.

I stayed close to Jacky. We did a lot together. Her family owned the local hardware store. I thought I loved her. Most of our time alone was spent kissing. We were both virgins and neither of us really knew what to do next. I was accepted in her home and grew to really like her family. I was never comfortable with them, though. I felt like I was on the outside looking in, as if her parents were expecting her to come to her senses and realize that she could do better – a lot better.

There were times when I felt I would never live to see sixteen. Then, once I did, I thought I would die at eighteen. I even went so far as to tell Jacky that doctors predicted I wouldn't live much longer. All I wanted was her attention. And I would do anything to get it.

I was already on the wrong road, seeking the wrong things. Life would have been much easier for me if I'd made a few simple little changes. I just didn't know what changes to make.

> ***Seek ye first the kingdom of God.***
> **(Matthew 6:33)**

At the time, New York State's legal drinking age was eighteen. All I had to do to get beer was have an eighteen-year-old friend, or brother of a friend, get it for me.

When the older high schoolers wanted to drink, they went to a well-known area in Williamsville called Beer Can Alley. It was located alongside Ellicott Creek. I spent many drunken nights there, wasting time, thinking I was enjoying myself, not realizing that my time there was just more of my life that didn't matter.

We never really had much else to do with our time, it seemed. Besides, I figured it was harmless. And after all, "everyone" was doing it.

On one of our drunken evenings after a visit to Beer Can Alley, some of my friends and I stopped at the local drug store. Not realizing how drunk we were, we gave the pharmacist a hard time. He called the police, and before we knew it we were surrounded. The druggist pointed me out as the lead troublemaker. What can I say? I just had a way about me. Of course, the fact that I was going to walk out without paying for a baseball bat and ball could have had something to do with it.

When one of the police officers questioned me, my drunken logic took over and I asked him, "What do I have to do to get out of this, hire the television attorney, Perry Mason?"

He arrested me for refusing to cooperate. I was held at the police station until my mother rescued me.

It didn't take long for my case to make it to juvenile court, where I was given a choice by the judge: Either go to military school or get put into a juvenile correctional facility.

Since I'd enjoyed playing with soldiers when I was young, I figured military school probably wouldn't be all that bad.

I also figured that military school would give me a clean start. Nothing seemed to be going right for me at Williamsville High anyway. *Besides*, I thought, *I'll get to wear a uniform every day!*

The Struggle to Find Meaning

Cardinal Farley Military Academy in Rhinecliff, New York, was my destination . . . or was that destiny? I agreed to repeat my freshman year there in order to enroll. It was a six- to eight-hour train ride with a change in Albany. I hoped—and I'm sure the judge, police, and my parents did as well—that it was far enough from Williamsville to do me some good.

The ruling order at Cardinal Farley was called the Christian Brothers of Ireland. They seemed like a strict bunch, but I was ready for anything.

I thought at first that I would meet a lot of very straight cadets there. After all, who else would want to go to military school besides smart children of wealthy families? But once I started meeting my classmates, I discovered that my bad attitude and troubled life were nothing compared to the problems some of those kids faced.

Many had divorced parents; some had no visitors at all throughout the school year. A few had committed crimes, including car theft, assault and battery, breaking and entering, and even armed robbery. I was definitely small time compared to them.

My life did seem to get better. I didn't have much contact with the outside world, and the brothers made us go to church a lot.

On rare occasions when we went to see movies in town, all hell would break loose. Somehow the local girls would find out when we were coming, and many would turn out in hopes of catching one of those rich cadets. Many cadets fell in love with the strangest-looking girls. In a dark movie theater in a faraway town, the rules of attraction change.

I'd only been at Cardinal Farley for a couple of months when the Cuban Missile Crisis hit in October 1962. We were all taken to the chapel to say confession and wait for word of war. There were a lot of nervous moments over those thirteen days. I thought we'd all be called to fight.

"If the government needed us to fight in that war, we'd lose," I told a friend. We were just a bunch a losers from all over the country.

Even though I had priests and brothers around me all the time, I never really cared much about God. He was out there somewhere in the distance, and it seemed like nobody really knew how to get in touch with Him. Certainly not me.

At the end of the day, the brothers enjoyed their own fun nights. While we cadets were safely tucked in bed, the brothers would stay up until all hours, drinking and singing Irish folk songs. We spent many sleepless nights wishing they would shut up and go to bed.

My brother, Louis, also attended Cardinal Farley. My sister, Joanne, was back in Williamsville, finishing her Catholic high school days. I was never sure which one of us had the tougher deal.

When Louis and I had some holidays off, we traveled by train back to Buffalo, along with two or three other cadets from the city. We had eight hours to kill, and most of that time was spent in the train's club car, drinking cocktails.

On one trip back to school, we had to change trains in Albany. We'd all had a few too many drinks during our three-hour lay-over. Everyone ran back to catch the train except for two of us. We had met female nursing students at the station and they wanted to show us their apartment. *Wow,* I thought. *This is it! Good-bye, virginity!* My friend scored that night. I didn't.

We were so drunk that my girl passed out on the floor and I passed out on a chair. My friend and I caught the next day's train and walked into the military academy a full day late. No one said much to us about it. We told the principal we'd missed the train in Albany and had no other choice but to stay over. I never thought about the fact that Louis made it back on time.

I guess I should have known that things had gone too smoothly and that I couldn't have gotten away that clean.

Military School's Loss Is Williamsville's Gain

I told everyone I'd scored with the Albany nursing student. The dean heard about it through the grapevine and I was finally punished for being AWOL.

That year ended uneventfully. It seemed that every year—every month, week, or even day, for that matter—ended without much to show for it. I don't know what I expected life to be like. I guess I thought every day should be filled with wildness and fun times . . . or at least some excitement.

When our break ended after the summer of 1963, my father received word that his son Martin was no longer welcome at Cardinal Farley.

Rejected by the losers! In that small group of kids who'd been tossed into a special school because they couldn't manage their lives elsewhere, I wasn't even good enough to be one of the rejects.

But I didn't think of it that way. Instead, I turned my back on them all. *Who needs it anyway?* I thought.

My father appealed and finally convinced them to give me another chance. I didn't really want to go back, but I promised my parents I would try harder my second year.

The sophomore year at Cardinal Farley was predictable. Most of my old troublemaker buddies were back and we knew all the ropes. *Nothing like old friends to dream up some fun,* I thought.

We looked forward to the trips to town. We were a year older and had a good shot at some of the girls. There were more girls to choose from too. But again, nothing materialized for me. Seniors and juniors got the best-looking girls. We got the popcorn and Cokes and picked on the freshmen.

I started stealing money from the school supply store, called the canteen. Other students had done it before me. They showed me how to loosen the metal exhaust grate in front of the store and create enough space to reach in and open the cash box and grab some money. I did this little crime three times.

I don't remember how much money I got away with, but the brothers caught on that the box was missing money. When everyone else was off at church one morning, I went to the store, not knowing that one of the brothers had spent the night there, waiting for the thief. Caught red-handed! I probably had about three dollars in change on me.

In August '64, just before I was supposed to go back for my third year, my dad got another letter from Cardinal Farley Military Academy. It said the same thing the first one had. "Martin will not be allowed back." My dad gave up. I was back in Williamsville for high school.

Ashamed? Remorseful? Me? "It's great to be back on old stomping grounds," I told myself.

But deep down inside I hurt. I covered the pain well, but I felt lost inside. The tough attitude I maintained looked good, but underneath that thick skin, I was sinking deeper in my own quicksand. I had the same feelings of sorrow and guilt that others had. But by continuing to bury those feelings instead of learning to deal with them, I was just delaying trouble.

Even worse, the pain was building. I was like a simmering volcano of emotion that would someday erupt.

I had no way of knowing when.

Love's Mystery and Misery

I liked getting away from the real

world when I was young. One of my favorite pastimes in my teen years was listening to music. I spent hours sitting in front of my parents' stereo, listening to records. I fantasized about being in a rock 'n' roll band, performing in front of thousands of screaming fans. Even when I was supposed to be doing homework, I was really just sitting at my desk pretending I was driving a car with the radio blasting.

Williamsville High wasn't a great place for me, either. I quit every sport I tried out for. I hated to practice. Other things were always more important. Especially after I met Patti.

She told me she was a virgin, but she seemed too experienced. She'd come to Williamsville from Fillmore High in New York City, which was far enough away that I had no way of finding out if she was telling the truth. And after a while, it didn't matter. I was in love!

We spent many long hours in a local motel room discovering each other. For two whole weeks while my parents were out of town, I skipped school completely. I had a friend call the high school and tell them I was sick.

During those two weeks, it finally happened. I was no longer a virgin. Wow! It sure felt great to be in love. *This is really living,* I thought. But I still had so much to learn.

My first physical pains of love came in the form of little creatures with many legs. It happened about four weeks after I met Patti. The little guys itched a lot and dug their way into my skin. I didn't know what they were, so I picked one up and brought it to my business teacher.

"Man, you have the crabs," he yelled after taking one look at the creature. "Get away from me!" I had never heard the word *crabs* before, so his reaction didn't bother me. At least I knew they had a name.

When I asked a friend if he had ever heard of the crabs, he laughed and told me they were usually transferred from one person to another through sexual contact.

"Sexual contact?" I argued. "But Patti couldn't have gotten them from someone else and passed them on to me. Both of us were virgins."

I started having terrible pains when I urinated. I again found myself in a state of shock. *What have I got now?* I wondered. *Cancer?*

My doctor told me I didn't have cancer, but the clap—slang for gonorrhea.

"But my girlfriend and I were both virgins. It's impossible for me to have the clap."

38

I realized Patti wasn't being honest with me about being a virgin. I thought love was all about trust and honesty. I wanted to love and be loved and have an honest relationship. It looked like I was off to a wrong start.

Will I ever get this right? It seemed so easy for other people. *I must be missing something. Something important.*

> **Seek ye first the kingdom of God, and his righteousness; and all these things shall be added unto you.**
> **(Matthew 6:33)**

The Politics of Death and Parties

I never cared much for politics while in high school. I didn't know the difference between Democrats and Republicans, and I didn't care.

I was in history class on November 22, 1963, when President John F. Kennedy was assassinated. When it was announced over the loudspeaker, my history teacher sat on his desk and started weeping.

After class, some of us treated it like a joke. "One down and one to go," I said, referring to Vice President Lyndon Johnson.

Nothing seemed to matter much to me. The president of the United States had been shot to death, and there I was joking around.

The assassination finally sank in after I got home and found the television networks all covering the story from morning to night. I felt the weight of it then and I got wrapped up in trying to understand who had committed the crime of killing the president. Those broadcasts laid the foundation for my distrust of government, as they did for many other Americans.

I became a follower of assassination theories. To this day, I am still a sucker for a new book on the subject.

The assassination and the events that followed affected me, but still not too deeply. I didn't take part in any protests or join a commune. I was still "Party Marty."

Most weekends I hosted "all you can drink" beer parties in my parents' backyard while they were out. I bought a few kegs and charged people a dollar each for all they could drink. I even hired a local band to perform. People came from all over. Sometimes I didn't know half the people there. But one thing was sure: I always had plenty of money in my pocket the next day.

Sometimes my parents went on vacation for a week or two. My party would start as soon as they left for the airport and end about an hour before they came in the door.

40

At every party, we drank gallons of beer, wine, whiskey, and hard cider. By the end of the evening, people would be sleeping throughout the house. As soon as we all came to, the party resumed.

My high school career didn't end the conventional way. I spent my final months of school in the hospital. I got another case of the clap and decided to try to heal myself. Since I worked at a drug store, I swiped some penicillin and kept it in the glove compartment of my car for more than a week before I got up the nerve to ask one of my coworkers to give me a shot of it. I didn't know it was important to keep the medicine refrigerated.

Later that day, I developed a high fever and swelled up like a balloon. My mother rushed me to the hospital. While there, I noticed that I had more of those little creatures biting me again.

When June came, I didn't walk across the stage like the other graduates, but I did finish high school. They mailed me my diploma. It was just like the rest of my high school days, out of step with the other kids.

The only thing I seemed to have a handle on was throwing parties and entertaining. I didn't realize it at the time, but I was laying the foundation for a career that would last for almost two decades.

Chapter 4
Reaching for Help

Graduating from high school didn't give me any more direction or purpose. As I continued to recover from my health problems, I kept throwing parties and living it up. Hardly good preparation to start college in the fall. Still, I enrolled at the Rochester Institute of Technology. Why? I was finished with high school; college seemed like the next logical step.

One of my first mistakes was buying a portable television set my first week in school. While everyone else studied, I watched my favorite programs. "Don't you think you should do without TV while in college?" a fellow student asked me. My response: "Don't you think you should mind your own business?"

I knew better, right? I had it all under control.

But the lack of interest in studying and the other competing influences in my life combined to doom my college career, fast. I didn't make it past the first semester.

During what would have been my second semester at Rochester, I joined the Spring Break flock on the annual migration to Fort Lauderdale. A friend and I stayed at one of the many hotels that were filled with college students on vacation.

We stayed drunk the whole time and I wound up getting arrested by the police for being drunk and disorderly. I was just sitting in front of the hotel. I didn't think I was doing anything wrong. But I was indeed drunk, so my reality was hazy at best.

I spent the night in the Fort Lauderdale jail, along with about two hundred other drunken students. This was the notorious jail made famous by the '60s beach movie, *Where the Boys Are*.

I was so bad, the police threw me into the drunk tank. I awakened with a tremendous hangover and a bum trying to put his hand in my pocket and take whatever he could find. I screamed at him, "Get away from me, you drunk."

The judge released me the next day . . . after I paid a $50 fine. When I returned to the hotel, I was hailed as a hero. Everyone accepted me. And I liked the recognition. I was cool! I was accepted for being drunk and breaking the law. What a claim to fame!

I returned to Rochester and dropped out of school. I then moved back to Buffalo where I continued to have trouble with the law. My difficulties with the local police force were only minor, but I was developing quite a reputation. More often than not, if a cop was driving down the street and saw me coming in the opposite direction, he would turn his car around and follow me just to see where I was headed. Eventually, I took back roads in and out of town to avoid the police.

I realize now that I wasn't avoiding just the police. I was avoiding God too.

The Roots of Rebellion

No longer attending college in Rochester, I enrolled at a local business college in downtown Buffalo, New York. The big attraction for this school was that it was close to Frank and Teresa's Anchor Bar, the place that made Buffalo chicken wings famous. I spent many class hours there with my friends, drinking beer and eating wings.

The late 1960s seemed like one big mess. The Vietnam War was escalating and the US continued to increase its participation. Everyone was concerned about being drafted and going off to fight a war that we didn't understand.

It was during a lecture in English class that I first heard a dissenting remark about the war. My professor was strongly against it, and he made sure all his students knew where he stood.

I had seen TV news reports of demonstrations protesting the war. I'd heard that the local police used tear gas to break up a demonstration at the University of Buffalo. But that all seemed distant from me. I never thought the radical element would take hold at a business college.

I started to smoke pot around that time. I bought my first $5 bag during one of my breaks in class. It was all seeds, but I didn't know what it was supposed to be. I crushed the seeds and rolled them into a joint and smoked it with my friend. Nothing much happened, though. I certainly didn't feel high.

"Not much to this pot business," I told my friend. He said he was going to see a friend for some real weed. He came back with a big joint that we smoked in barely a minute. We held our breath for what seemed like hours. Finally, we started giggling and eating anything we could get our hands on. We were thankful to have "chicken wing heaven" right near the school.

I experimented with various other drugs at this time too. I tried a heart drug called amyl nitrite (commonly known as "poppers"). It smelled like dirty socks but it made me laugh uncontrollably for several minutes right after inhaling it. One day, in math class, I opened about ten glass capsules of the stuff at one time, within a few feet of my professor's desk. He got a funny look on his face when he took a whiff of the aroma. At first he laughed. But after he recovered and figured out who had done it, he threw me out of class.

My English professor had a tremendous influence on me. He got through to me by really talking to me and listening to what I had to say. Other professors only seemed to talk *at* me. He brought in all sorts of books for me to read. Most of them were really radical. Maybe that's what made them so interesting.

While the war raged in Vietnam, not much seemed normal in the US. As protests increased on college campuses and inner cities across the country, student deferments were taken away from draft-eligible young men.

I protested the war because everyone else I knew did. I didn't know why we were fighting it in the first place, but my professor filled in a lot of the blanks. After hearing his views, I believed with all my being that the war was wrong. I didn't want to have any part in it. I got so radical I began to demonstrate everything and anything.

Students from my school joined in with the rest of the American colleges and started to protest the war. So I filled my time by organizing demonstrations. I also became a spokesperson. I made up signs and marched around the front of the administration building with a handful of fellow students. We thought we had meaning and purpose. My English professor came to each rally, and he looked thrilled to be there. But he never marched with us.

The business college expelled me — not for grades, but for the protests. *I guess business college just isn't ready for me,* I thought.

I started spending a lot of time hanging around the University of Buffalo. I was accepted among all the radical students there, and I felt I'd found a purpose in life.

I attended many Students for a Democratic Society rallies and found acceptance there. I got caught up in the movement, even though I didn't fully understand it.

I didn't know what the definition of *radical* was. I didn't find out until years later, when I was in my thirties. At the time, I figured everyone was that way. If you weren't fighting against the war, you must be for the war. And that certainly wasn't cool.

Why should I further my education anyway? I asked myself. *We're all going to die in a nuclear war. This must be the end of the world!*

Matters of Life and Death

There was a lot of fear on campus in those days, but no one cared. It was "us against them." I didn't really have any idea who "them" was. *Maybe it's our parents,* I thought. Many rally speakers and war protesters called the enemy the "establishment."

"What in the world is the 'establishment'?" I asked. I never got a straight answer. But I soon started believing it was anyone who wasn't with us. If you were not against the Vietnam War, you were considered the establishment.

The assassinations of Martin Luther King and Robert F. Kennedy deeply affected my rebellion. I found life extremely confusing, and I met many people who felt the same way. In fact, thousands of us were desperately trying to find the meaning of life. None of us really knew the facts behind what our government was doing, but we were all in the same boat.

I found it impossible to believe in our country anymore and became part of the Students for a Democratic Society, a new movement that was spreading across the nation. We all had the same cause. I could never really explain exactly what the cause was, but it had a lot to do with the "us vs. them" perspective.

While demonstrating at the University of Buffalo—not attending classes, of course—I started getting involved in promoting rock concerts on campus. The groups appeared to support our cause. The music seemed secondary to the speaker, who always spoke out against everything our country stood for.

Rock music added fuel to the fire raging within me. The message was always the same: Tune in and drop out! Tune in to the subculture and drop out of mainstream society. I became more rebellious with each breath, and now had something to blame it on: society.

When I heard that the only way to get out of serving in Vietnam was to get married, I proposed to Susan, who was my girlfriend at the time. We'd met at a dance and fell instantly in love. We both believed in the same causes. I was twenty-one; she was nineteen. The marriage didn't last very long and we divorced four years later. But not before we had two beautiful daughters, Brigitte and Michelle.

Life Goes On

I started playing piano in a band. But I never quite got the hang of it. So I gave up and started managing a local band called the Rising Sons. The irony didn't hit me until much later in life that the band I managed in those years had a name that is often used to describe Jesus Christ, the Son of God, raised from death.

The Rising Sons changed their name to the Raven and started playing at the Glen Park Casino, Buffalo's top nightspot. Whenever a big band came to town, my band opened for them.

Those musicians had some serious talent. I thought they had the potential to become big stars. Several of the musicians in out-of-town bands, who were hired as head-liners, shook in their shoes after hearing them. Some didn't want to even take the stage after Raven finished their set. The Raven was good, but they needed exposure outside Buffalo.

All the up-and-coming bands were drug groups. We were straight-looking young boys from Buffalo, just experimenting with smoking pot. The Raven had plenty of raw talent, but no record deal

So I started traveling back and forth to New York City to set up bookings and expose the group to the world.

Chapter 5
Livin' the Dream

Unlike my personal life, work was turning out pretty good for me. On one of my trips to New York City as a rock 'n' roll manager, I went to a nightclub called the Scene.

The Scene was where bands came to wind down after playing weekend concerts at Fillmore East. That was the major concert nightspot in New York City at the time. It was an old movie theater that Bill Graham had converted into a concert hall. Every young aspiring musician and every major rock 'n' roll band in the world wanted to make it onto Graham's stage.

The bands always brought their groupies, crew, and managers to the Scene with them. Agents, producers, and media followed too. The average entourage numbered around twenty. If Bill Graham booked two or three opening acts, the Scene would be filled to capacity just with people from the music industry. Fans lined up for hours to get a glimpse of their favorite stars. Some nights, the place was so crammed, it seemed not one more person could be shoehorned in. But if you had a big enough name, the owner, Steve Paul, always found room.

Steve was picky about who could play at the Scene. He had the hottest club in town, so he had a reputation to live up to. Since he could make or break a group just by exposing them to his audience, he wanted only top-name bands, or at the very least, an up-and-coming group.

The Raven wasn't a top-name band then, but one night, as the club was packed and rocking, I approached Steve and asked, "Would you be interested in booking a great band from Buffalo?"

"Get a hit record," he hollered over the loud music. "Then come back and see me."

Hit record? *Sure, I carry them in my pocket*. Obviously, that wasn't going to happen. So I started searching the Scene for someone who might be interested in my band.

Just as I began looking around, Jimi Hendrix walked by. *The* Jimi Hendrix! There he was, the man most people believed to be the greatest guitar player of all time. *That is,* I thought proudly, *until the music world hears John Weitz, the Raven's lead guitarist.*

All I needed was to come up with the nerve to talk to this rock 'n' roll legend. I wasn't much for speaking up for myself, so my approach had to be quick and to the point. Before I could lose my courage, I stopped him. "Jimi," I said, "would you be interested in listening to a tape of a really hot group?"

Fully expecting a quick "No way," I was shocked when he said, "Sure, why not? I'm always ready to listen to new bands. But this place is beginning to get to me, so let's cut back to Steve's office. I'm sure he won't mind."

I gulped. "Listen, Jimi," I said, feeling nervous, "Steve said he isn't interested in what I have to offer, so I'm not sure he'd be too happy to see me in his office."

"Don't worry about it, man," Jimi said with a grin. "You're in good hands. Now, let's go listen to your tape."

Was I dreaming? There I was, walking to Steve Paul's office with Jimi Hendrix. It was too good to be true!

I set up the reel-to-reel tape recorder I hauled around with me. Portable cassette players weren't used for professional music back then, so my twenty-pound Panasonic had to do.

I told Jimi I had three songs on my

tape and would appreciate it if he would listen to them all.

"Let's get through the first one before I commit to the others," he said. "But first, let's get stoned."

Stoned? Wow. I was going to get high with one of the world's most famous musicians. I was going to party with the big boys at Steve Paul's Scene. I had made it!

I answered. "But I don't have any grass with me."

"Don't worry," he said. "My friend has a stash of super killer weed with him. I'll go get him."

Jimi bolted out the door and returned with his friend and a couple of groupies.

Joints were passed around the room. Everyone got a full hit and held it for what seemed like forever.

Jimi walked in front of me, with a joint held backward in his closed mouth, motioning me to get ready for a shotgun blast. I had never had a shotgun blast of pot. I wasn't one for placing my lips on a stranger's, especially not another man's. *I don't care if it is Jimi Hendrix,* I thought, *I'm not letting him near my lips.*

But before I could even finish the thought, Hendrix shotgunned me. I almost choked!

No one will ever believe this, I

thought. Then I wondered, *Is this what making it in the music business is all about?* It seemed odd. But who was I to question?

After everyone was high, I stumbled to the tape machine and started the first song. The music blasted out of the speakers and sounded great. Everyone got into the beat. Soon Jimi started singing along and clapping to the tempo.

When the song ended, Jimi yelled, "This group is great! Keep that tape moving, Marty."

Just then, in walked Steve Paul. He looked right at me. "What are you doing here? I thought I told you to come back when you had a hit record."

"Steve," Hendrix said, "you have to book this band. I want to see them perform live here. The Raven is one of the best groups I've ever heard, and I've only listened to one song."

Steve sat down and we all listened to the rest of the tape and drank a bottle of cognac. Jimi asked to hear the tape again and we spent the next hour partying and listening to the Raven.

This was the life. Partying with celebrities, listening to rock 'n' roll, tasting success. What more could I possibly want?

There is a way which seemeth right

> *unto a man, but the end thereof are*
> *the ways of death.* **(Proverbs 14:12)**

On the Way

From that day on, I had a different relationship with Steve Paul. He immediately booked the Raven at the Scene.

Steve would never have considered the group without Hendrix's stamp of credibility. He needed someone else to tell him what was good or bad. That was the attitude of most people in the music business. The musicians knew who was really good. Most business people were just along for the ride.

I was on a different ride. I was starting to make it. And I was going to make it big. I was following my instincts and they were paying off. The life I'd been seeking was finally going to happen.

If only I had sought the right life.

> *Seek ye first the kingdom of God,*
> *and his righteousness; and all these*
> *things shall be added unto you.*
> **(Matthew 6:33)**

Turn Up the Volume

The Raven had been endorsed by none other than Jimi Hendrix, and they'd been booked at the Scene. But what would happen once they got on stage? Could they really pull this off? If anything went wrong, Steve Paul would run me out of town.

The band came through with flying colors. The Raven's first appearance at the Scene impressed everyone who heard them. The rock musicians in the club sat in their seats all night with their mouths wide open.

Steve Paul told me that after the band finished its first set, Bobby Columby, drummer for the popular group Blood, Sweat & Tears, came up to him and asked, "Who are these guys?" He told Steve he came in to have a few drinks and meet some women. "I didn't expect to be turned around like this," he said. "The guy on drums is phenomenal."

I knew it! I knew it! I knew it! I screamed inside.

But on the outside, I just smiled with satisfaction.

Performers from all over New York City came to see the Raven. Most musicians of the day, including the Who, the Grateful Dead, and Jefferson Airplane, were known for making a lot of noise and feedback from overpowered amplifiers. But the Raven was different. They didn't have to hide behind ear-splitting sound effects. Each musician had mastered his own instrument.

Most bands had one musician who stood out from the rest. Usually, it was the main guitar player, the lead vocalist, or the songwriter. Record companies catered to the band's one standout, who almost always wound up splitting from the group over petty jealousies. Those problems hadn't affected the Raven.

Once they hit the stage, things began to happen fast. The guys became the club's house band. Anyone who was anyone came to see them. Groups visiting New York had to go to the Scene to catch the exciting new band. Not a night went by without one or more famous rock stars in the audience. Many took turns sitting in with the Raven and jamming after their final set.

Positive feedback began pouring in for the Raven. "This group must be good if they attract this kind of response from the musicians," I heard a booking agent say to a friend.

After the shows, back in the dressing room, drugs and drinking ran rampant. All I could think was *This is the big time! I've got everything I ever wanted!*

So why did I still feel empty inside?

Of course I didn't realize it at the time, but the Bible had the answer to my question.

> *The works of the flesh are manifest, which are these; adultery, fornication, uncleanness, lascivious-*

*ness, idolatry, witchcraft, hatred,
variance, emulations, wrath, strife,
seditions, heresies, envyings, mur-
ders, drunkenness, revellings, and
such like ... shall not inherit the
kingdom of God.*

(Galatians 5:19-21)

Hanging On at the Start

As more musicians heard of the
Raven, I received calls from managers who
wanted to take over the group. Lew
Merninstein, manager for Van Morrison, contacted me. He showed serious interest in the
Raven, but wanted to be the manager. I
explained to him that it was not an option.
The Raven and I had been through a lot
together and I wasn't going to bow out on
the verge of success.

The only downside was that the band
appealed to musicians, but not to the average
person who was into rock 'n' roll. The Raven
was too complex and sophisticated for most
New Yorkers. So the band and I weren't
making much money. But we were having a
great time, partying and rubbing elbows with
the stars.

We moved from Buffalo to New
York and rented a house in Brooklyn. We
were getting closer to a recording contract.
We signed an exclusive booking contract

with Ira Blacker from Associated Booking, Inc. Ira loved the Raven's music and arranged for us to travel up and down the East Coast. Our travels spread wider as we became a regular act in Boston, Philadelphia, Detroit, Chicago, and finally back at the Fillmore East in Manhattan. We opened shows for headline groups like Led Zeppelin, the Byrds, Procol Harum, Chambers Brothers, Albert King, Richie Havens, John Mayall, Johnny Winter, the Rascals, Jethro Tull, and others.

The Raven also became accepted in the underground music movement.

Underground music was far outside the mainstream, even extreme among the hippie culture. The underground movement always had two elements at any rally: rock music and a radical speaker. We did rallies with Abby Hoffman and Jerry Rubin, two well-known members of the Chicago Seven, the group accused of organizing the riots at the 1968 Democratic National Convention in Chicago.

When the Beatles started their own label, Apple Records, I took a bold step and sent in a tape. Unbelievably, I received a telegram from George Harrison himself, saying he wanted to sign the Raven and produce our first album!

News of Harrison's interest spread

quickly through the music business. Soon we had offers from just about every music company in the country.

"We want the Raven," RCA Records said. Just a few months before, no one there would even return my phone calls. Atlantic Records, MGM, Capital, Electra, Columbia, and many independent producers wanted a piece of the action. Even Jimi Hendrix's business partner Eddie Kramer wanted to produce the group at Jimi's new Electric Ladyland recording studios.

Nothing could stop us now, I thought. We were headed straight to the top. John Lennon had said the Beatles were more popular than Jesus Christ. But we were about to become more popular than the Beatles!

Success was dead ahead. I could taste it. Getting to the top would fix every other problem I had, right? Right?

More popular than Jesus Christ . . .

Did Somebody Say Woodstock?

George Harrison arranged to meet us in Los Angeles, so we loaded up two vans of equipment and drove to LA. We waited there for nearly a month, then found out that Harrison was going into the hospital to have his teeth fixed. I couldn't believe it! We'd driven three thousand miles to meet with him and he goes into the hospital for oral surgery!

To make matters worse, rumor had it the Beatles were splitting up. If that happened, no one could guarantee Apple Records would stay in business.

We returned to New York. I asked our agent, Ira Blacker, to seek a deal with another company.

Ira advised us to consider signing with a more established record company. He suggested Columbia Records, who was very interested in us.

But I still wanted to find out what George Harrison wanted to do. Peter Asher came out to meet with me. He was the brother of Jane Asher, who was then Paul McCartney's girlfriend, though they were splitting up at the time. I met with him at the Scene.

Peter explained that George Harrison was still recovering from surgery. "So the Beatles want me to produce the Raven for Apple Records," he said.

I asked Peter if he knew anything about producing records. He said he did, and in fact was once a member of the group Peter and Gordon. He wasn't very convincing. I didn't like his style and he certainly didn't have Harrison's name. I figured even if the Beatles did split up, I at least wanted Harrison associated with the first Raven album. But Asher said it would either be him or no deal. I discussed his offer with the members of the band and we said no deal.

Peter Asher went on to produce huge hits for Linda Ronstadt, Neil Diamond, Cher, Diana Ross, Kenny Loggins, James Taylor, and others.

We contacted our lawyer, Miles Laurie, who set up a meeting with Columbia Records. But by this time, the Raven wasn't the hot item it once was. We'd wasted too much time trying to get the Apple Records deal with Harrison.

Miles Laurie represented a lot of famous people in the music business, including artists such as Ray Charles and Barry Manilow. Before our meeting with Columbia Records, he set up a meeting with Michael Lang.

Michael was one of the organizers and producers of the 1969 Woodstock Music Festival. He told me that if we signed a contract with him to be Raven's producer, he would allow them to play at his music festival.

I told Michael I didn't think Raven would be interested in playing Woodstock. We were there in '68, as the first electric band ever to play Woodstock. Before '69, the annual event was strictly for acoustic groups, and the folk people were still trying to recover from Bob Dylan's departure from

65

that scene. The organizers made us wait till the very last minute before they put my group on. Once the Raven hit the stage, they were booed and disrespected by the audience. It certainly was not worth signing a production contract just to be a part of the '69 festival.

Michael said this year's festival was going to be different. His was special. *Special?* I wondered. *How would his festival be any different from any other Woodstock Music Festival?* I discussed Lang's offer with the band and we turned him down.

The Raven finally signed a recording contract with Columbia Records. It wasn't what we'd all expected, but at least an album was going to be recorded, released, and promoted.

Columbia was the largest record company in the world, and being a part of their family was supposed to be an honor. It didn't have the hype of George Harrison, I thought, but we needed to get on with things.

I did get on with things. Just not the right things.

Chapter 6
Showtime

The pressure of making it in the big time takes a toll on everyone. Members of the Raven and their families were not immune.

The musicians began fighting fiercely among themselves, especially about which songs to include on the album. Each member insisted on having his original tune included. But each member had a completely different style. The mix was country, blues, jazz, and ballads. There was no Raven style of original material, no Raven sound, just a mix of everything.

Looking back on it, I'm reminded of the story of the Tower of Babel as described in Genesis chapter 11. Speaking one language, the people could have built a structure that reached to the heavens. But God knew that if they succeeded, nothing would be impossible for them, and they wouldn't learn anything while on earth. So He confused their language, and eventually they couldn't understand one another any longer. So they couldn't possibly build their tower.

The Raven could have made the big time. They should have been hugely successful. But what would the band members have learned? What would I have learned? We would have had success and fame, maybe fortune too. But at what cost?

Janis Joplin, the famous rock and blues singer, was so impressed with the Raven's sound that when the band played at Ungano's Night Club in Manhattan she arrived with her entire band . . . and three professional tape recorders. That didn't go over well with the Raven, and they insisted I tell Janis to turn off the recorders.

I asked club owner Nick Ungano to step in. He didn't want to mess with Janis. She had a well-earned reputation for being loud and obnoxious, bordering on anger every second—especially when she drank Southern Comfort, her favorite booze. And she always drank Southern Comfort, onstage and off. When I reminded Nick that we had a contract that didn't allow tape recorders, he agreed to approach Janis. We all expected the worst.

We were not disappointed.

Of course Nick blamed the entire

fiasco on me. He told her that the Raven's manager demanded that she turn off the tape recorders or the group wouldn't go on stage.

"Manager?" she screamed. Then she exploded with a barrage of profanity, insisting that Nick tell me to do something to myself that was a physical impossibility.

I went over to Janis's table and tried to smooth things over. She didn't appreciate my presence and let me know in no uncertain terms what she thought of me. But I explained to her that the Raven was only worried about having tapes of their songs floating around before they released their own album.

"Put yourself in our place," I suggested to her.

She told me we should consider it a compliment to be taped by her. I told her I agreed, but that didn't change anything. The tape recorders had to go.

They did, and so did Janis Joplin, who stormed out in front of a full house.

But no one in the Raven really cared what Janis thought or did.

"She should consider it a privilege to be sitting in the club listening to us," said Tommy Calandra, our bass guitarist. "Joplin's just looking for a new sound. But it's not going to be ours. Let her wait until we have an album out and she can buy it like everyone else."

Janice and I became friends a few months later, after introducing her to organist Richard Kermode. Joplin quit her original band, Big Brother and the Holding Company, and was putting together her own group and needed musicians. She tried to hire Raven pianist Jim Calire, but later settled for Kermode.

After Columbia released the Raven's self-titled album in August 1969—which should have been the band's big break—the group moved back to Buffalo. We figured if we could travel around the country out of New York City, we could travel from our hometown just as well. It would certainly be easier on the group's families.

But it really didn't matter where we lived. Place wasn't the problem. The band was the problem. Nobody liked one another anymore. On the verge of stardom, the group split up.

OK, This Is the Bottom, Right?

While I was shepherding the Raven through the breakup, my personal life was a mess too. Steve Morrow, a longtime friend, had a religious experience while taking LSD. He said he found Jesus Christ and started reading the Bible every waking minute. I wanted to have the same kind of faith that

Steve seemed to have, but I could never quite understand it.

I smoked pot and read the Bible while driving in the group van. I thought I had a close relationship with God. I even marked my Bible with insights that came to me. But one entry summed up my overall feeling about it: "This Bible is very hard to understand. Try smoking a joint before you study it."

While reading the book of Revelation I became fascinated by the 666 beast remarks. I even convinced Tommy Calandra to write a song titled "The Persuader," based entirely on Revelation 13:18: *"Here is wisdom. Let him that hath understanding count the number of the beast: for it is the number of a man; and his number is six hundred threescore and six."*

I didn't really know who or what the beast was back then. I didn't even know what salvation was. I was still living for the moment, with no real plan for my life. I couldn't figure out how God wanted me to behave. The pain and disappointment I'd lived through to that point in my life didn't seem to matter. I still had much to learn. And because I wasn't living the way I should, or listening to God's voice, I would end up learning the hard way.

I moved into a house in an area near

Buffalo named Clarence. The house was a duplex and I had the downstairs. I enjoyed country living. It sure was better than Brooklyn.

My band-managing career had been derailed—whether temporarily or permanently, I couldn't know at the time. But my life continued to revolve around smoking pot and hash. I'd met plenty of drug dealers through the music business, and I made it a point to stay in touch with them. I arranged to have drugs sent to me wherever I was.

One day, a friend and I ordered some hashish from a friend named Stan in New York. A few days later, when I walked down the long driveway to my mailbox on the street, I found a small package wrapped in psychedelic colors.

I glanced around to make sure no one saw me take the colorful package out of my mailbox. What was Stan thinking, sending drugs through the post office in such obvious packaging!

I brought the package inside as stealthily as I could, then called my friend to tell him it had arrived.

Two minutes after the call, I saw about two dozen uniformed police officers racing up my driveway. I ran into the bathroom and started to flush the hash down the toilet. But living in the country, I had septic tanks for sewage and the pressure was always low. So of course, one of the two pieces of hash came floating back up about the time the police broke down my front door. They went immediately to the bathroom.

Busted!

They arrested me and took me before a local judge. I was sent to county jail and had to be bailed out by my parents.

News of my arrest hit the local papers. I figured one good thing would come of this: at least the drug subculture would further accept my band and me. But this wasn't New York City. The subculture in our little community wasn't near as hip as in major cities.

Besides, I didn't have a band anymore.

Elton Who?

No more Raven, no more hanging out with stars like Jimi Hendrix, no more wheeling and dealing with legends like George Harrison. No more big time . . . at least for now. I was on my own again.

Or so I thought. Just like the many times before in my life, God was right there with me during those difficult moments. And He was ready to make the hard times much easier. All I had to do was ask. My Bible-reading taught me a little about Jesus, but I didn't know that He was there all the time, waiting for me to come to Him. And even if I did, I wouldn't know how to ask for His help.

> *Behold, I stand at the door, and knock: if any man hear my voice, and open the door, I will come in to him, and will sup with him, and he with me.* **(Revelation 3:20)**

I used my contacts in the music business to book bands in and around Buffalo. Booking agents were always looking for ways to expose their clients. One agent had Rod Stewart in town for a concert. Rod had promised to come to whatever club would host a particular unknown singer after his concert so he could party with this new guy.

I laughed when I found out the guy's name. "Who would ever come to see a performer with the name of Elton John?" Even if we got him for the $50 the agent was asking for, it wouldn't be worth it. Nobody knew him. "Sorry," I told the agent, "but people in Buffalo just aren't ready for a musician named Elton."

Wait! Didn't I Hit Bottom a Little While Ago?

I didn't realize it then, but I was searching for something in the music and bar scene. Maybe peace, maybe myself, maybe the right door to walk through.

If I'd been paying attention, I would have realized that what I was searching for was Jesus Christ. Without Him, my life was empty. I tried to fill the void with booze and drugs, something to ease my pain. But after the painkillers wore off, I felt terrible all over again . . . and worse because of the physical effects they brought on.

I couldn't come up with any relief for my pain. I told my friends and family that I needed a break from the music business. But I didn't really know what to do with myself or how to make a living any other way. I was stuck.

The lawyer who represented me during my hashish arrest suggested I move back to Buffalo. He had more connections in the city, and if I was ever arrested again, he could pull some strings.

This was a new strategy: a plan for handling my next arrest before it happened.

Having no better idea, I agreed to the move. Soon I'd be ready for one of three things: prison, a body bag, or the biggest change I could ever make.

Chapter 7
What's Next?

Following my lawyer's advice, I moved to Buffalo in April 1970. The pending drug case was dropped.

The fantasy of making it big in the rock 'n' roll business faded with each passing day. Life stunk.

"People think it's all lights, camera, and action," I told a friend. "They never really see what goes on day to day."

My life was as predictable as a yo-yo. Whenever I went into a rut, failed in a business venture, or messed up a relationship, I always climbed out and did well in whatever I tried next. That pattern was my curse . . . and my salvation.

When my father bought a retirement home in Fort Lauderdale, he met Jimmy Artis, a retired nightclub and restaurant owner from New Jersey. The two men struck up a friendship that led to a business partnership. My father became a silent partner in the Pizza Spot restaurant near the beach. He suggested I take a break from the music business and come to Fort Lauderdale to work with him. I thought it over and agreed that I needed to get away.

As soon as I arrived in Fort Lauderdale, I went to work as a partner at the Pizza Spot. It was about a block away from the beach, so we always had hungry customers with plenty of money.

Jimmy Artis and I hit it off right away, even though he was much older than I was. We took turns running the business. His wife, Terri, helped out a lot, so we men were free to party and promote.

We started to hang out at the Bachelors Three, a nightclub owned by football legend Joe Namath. The club was about two miles west of the Pizza Spot. I taught Jimmy Artis how to promote "Buffalo style" in a nightclub setting.

I'd learned the technique from the best in the business. Buffalo club owners knew how to promote new ventures. They went to competitors' clubs with five of their employees and bought drinks for everybody. They'd order fifty to a hundred screwdrivers (vodka and orange juice) all at once and pass them out. Of course, customers wanted to know who was buying drinks, and that gave the owners a chance to promote their new clubs.

This would go on for the entire evening, sometimes tying up bartenders for hours. The owners would leave a tip of a few hundred dollars and then move on to the next club to start the whole thing over again. This type of promotion attracted not only the club's customers but its employees as well.

Jimmy and I implemented this strategy at all of Fort Lauderdale's hot spots. Jimmy stuck close to the Bachelors because it had an older crowd, while I went to places like the Flying Machine, the Village Zoo, and the Parrot Lounge.

Our pizza business skyrocketed. Ah, sweet success! *Finally,* I thought, *I'm making big money.* I bought a new Jaguar XKE convertible. Three days later, Jimmy Artis did the same. His was yellow, mine was black. We had money to burn!

Some people, when they've gone through serious ups and downs, remember the bad times so they don't repeat them. Others—like me—don't. The yo-yo ride becomes an addiction as we try to grab the ups and hold on.

Nobody Gets Away for Free
Money is the answer to life and I

love it, I thought. *And I've got plenty!*

> **For the love of money is the root of all evil: which while some coveted after, they have erred from the faith, and pierced themselves through with many sorrows.**
> **(1 Timothy 6:10)**

I didn't realize it then, but the further I traveled down that godless path, the more difficult the road back would be . . . and the more likely it was that I wouldn't live to make it back. It took a long time for me to recognize that. And for someone who doesn't know Jesus Christ and His plan, that's the ultimate danger.

Looking back now, I can't believe how many times I went through the same cycles, endured the same experiences, without really growing or learning.

But I bet I'm not the only person guilty of that. When I look around now, I see people going through the motions, enduring an existence that's more of a routine than a life. They mindlessly go through each day, never even looking for a greater meaning.

At that point in my life, my biggest goal was making a lot of money and retiring at a young age. And I had plenty of chances.

Eventually tiring of the restaurant

business, my father and I decided to sell our share of the Pizza Spot to Jimmy. I wanted to get back into the nightclub scene. So I moved back to Buffalo.

I joined up with my friends Gus and Chick Driscetti. They had a couple of night clubs, and Chick ran one of them, Driscetti's, while Gus worked with their uncle Carlo at a bar Gus had designed called Dance Machine.

Chick asked if I wanted to be his partner in Driscetti's. I was looking for a quick way to make a living and had always wanted to own a bar, but my drug arrest kept me from getting a license. Working with Chick would be a good way to get into the business.

Life as a nightclub owner in Buffalo was a difficult existence. There was a bar on just about every corner.

Chick and I decided to remodel the club and change its name to Alexander's. On opening night, people came from miles around. Of course, Chick and I had been out promoting every night for at least three weeks before the opening.

People who went to bars in Buffalo liked to drink. That may sound obvious. But Buffalo people were different, at least back then (in the 1960s and '70s). They didn't just drink. They drank and drank and drank! Not one drink at a time, but ten or twenty. And they didn't like to drink alone.

Every night at Alexander's, we had some kind of special discount offer. That way, our customers could always get completely drunk yet still go home with money in their pockets.

I set up a deluxe sound system and had all the latest hits playing full blast all the time. People in Buffalo were getting used to having sound systems in bars. So my setup had to be the biggest and the best. I introduced the idea to Buffalo in 1969 at a club called Mulligan's Brick Bar, so I wanted to have the best one around. I spared no expense in building a state-of-the-art sound system with all the bells and whistles that were available at that time.

I loved getting behind the bar and serving booze. When customers came in alone, I always had a drink with them. Unfortunately, those customers wouldn't order just one drink. They'd get ten and expect me to drink ten with them.

There was no way I could spend that much time with each customer. So instead of having mixed drinks, I drank straight shots of whatever the customer was drinking. If a customer ordered ten screwdrivers, I drank ten shots of vodka.

I moved up and down the bar, drinking ten shots of whiskey with one customer and ten shots of scotch with another.

Many nights I made a complete fool of myself. One time I ripped the telephone off the wall and put it in the sink. More than once I stood behind the bar with my pants down to my ankles. I had to live up to my reputation as Party Marty, after all. I figured I had a responsibility to make sure my customers had a good time.

What was really happening was that my life was going downhill again . . . fast.

Sometimes I'd be so drunk by the time the bar closed that I couldn't see straight, let alone drive home. So I started spending the night in a little apartment in the back of the nightclub. If I did make it home, I would wake up in the morning, still completely dressed, on the floor outside my bedroom. What a life!

Doing My Thing

Running the bar had become much more than a way to make a living. I had turned into an alcoholic. But I didn't question my actions. I went along with the general attitude of the era: "If it feels good, do it!"

In 1972 I watched the movie *Superfly*. The film was about a Harlem drug pusher who wanted to get out of the business . . . but, of course, he had to do one last job first. I enjoyed every minute of that movie, and it made me long to try cocaine.

I purchased my first gram of coke when I was running Alexander's. The drug seemed to help me get through the night. I ran between the bar and the bathroom every fifteen minutes for a snort.

On many occasions, I split a supply of coke with a friend. I never thought of myself as a drug dealer.

Today, I consider myself extremely fortunate and blessed to still be around to tell my story. Any one of my drinking binges or cocaine parties could easily have put me six feet under. Yet because I survived my own selfishness and excess, I am now able to write this book. But how many people can't say that? How many aren't ready when the end comes up to meet them.

God's Plan Included John Lennon?

Sometimes I wonder about God's plan for our lives. It hasn't always been easy to believe that everything I went through was (and is) part of God's plan for me. Of course it wasn't God doing those things to me. It was me using my free will. But Jesus was always there for me, waiting for me to come to Him.

At that point in life, I wasn't thinking about going to God in any way, shape, or form. I wanted nothing to do with religion.

In 1972 I traveled back to Los Angeles, California. This time it was to see the undefeated Miami Dolphins play the Washington Redskins in the Super Bowl. I loved being back in LA! So much that I decided to stick around for a while.

I stayed with Gary Mallaber, former drummer with my old band, the Raven. We took a drive to Venice Beach one day and I liked what I saw. It reminded me of Florida.

I arranged to rent an apartment right on the beach. *This is living*, I thought. But I wasn't sure what I wanted to do with my life.

"Maybe I'll just retire," I said to Jessie Ed Davis, the famous Native American blues guitarist, whom I'd met through Gary.

"Why not?" Jessie said. "Life is great out here in California. There's always plenty of good dope and fine women. Life is a party. Go for it!"

Life is a party? Go for it? He was singing my tune!

I started drinking a bottle of booze a day and snorting a couple of grams. "Life is a party—Go for it!" became my life motto.

While I was visiting Jessie one day, John Lennon from the Beatles showed up with a small balloon in his hand. I was too stoned to be awed by the sudden appearance of one of the most famous people on earth. All I wanted to know was what that thing in his hand was.

"That, my friend, is some of the purest heroin in the world," he said.

Heroin? That was one thing I hadn't tried yet.

My first experience with heroin made me sick to my stomach. I wound up puking my guts out. But afterward I felt great.

"Wow!" I said. "This is the highest I've ever been. I actually feel . . . normal. Is that possible?"

"Sure, Marty," John said. "Look at me. Aren't I normal?"

Hanging out with famous rock stars was an unbelievable experience. Yet I still felt miserable inside. Deep down in my soul I was a wreck. I knew something was seriously wrong, but I couldn't figure out what it was that wasn't right.

My confusion led me into depression and despair. During one of my drunken and drugged stupors, a friend of mine from Buffalo warned me, "You're gonna get busted some day, Marty. They're watching you."

I didn't know what he was talking about. But the idea that somebody was looking over my shoulder at everything I did added paranoia to my already jumbled emotions.

Had I known at the time that my

friend Jessie was going to die of a heroin overdose, I might have been even more paranoid.

Chapter 8
Passing the Bar

In 1973, I decided to rent a house on Santa Monica Beach. I was still semi-retired, but stayed active in the music business . . . mainly in the party scene. I wasn't working with anyone in particular and was enjoying my freedom.

The beach house was fun, and the parties there lasted for weeks. Quaaludes were popular at the time, and I abused those heavily, along with plenty of booze. I stayed high for days on end. Balloons of heroin flowed freely.

The parties were great, but I was itching to get back to work. And I wanted to meet some new girls. So I got a job as a bartender at a place called the Boat Bar. This popular nightspot was located between Venice Beach and Santa Monica Beach.

On my first night, all my friends from the music business heard I was bartending, so they dropped by to party with me. I got so drunk I started acting like I owned the place. I gave away about a keg of beer and at least half a case of liquor. My tip jar overflowed.

At the end of the night, after all the customers had gone home, the owner of the Boat Bar asked me to come into his office. His first comment was "Did you know that we hire detectives to watch new employees for one week?"

I could tell from the look on his face that he was not pleased with the report he'd received.

"Look, sir," I said, "save it. I quit."

My job at the Boat Bar had lasted one night.

Love, Loss, and More Troubles

Valerie Sherman, a lady I'd met while running Alexander's in Buffalo, moved to California to live with her brother. I saw her when I went to her brother's weekly poker game, where a bunch of us smoked dope, snorted heroin, and played cards.

Valerie and I picked up right where we'd left off and soon fell in love. We rented a small apartment down the street from her brother.

Since I was still semi-retired, I had a lot of time on my hands. I spent my days getting high and watching the Watergate investigation on TV. I stayed glued to the set right up to and including President Nixon's resignation. I even called a telephone survey and voted to impeach him.

Not surprisingly, Valerie and I soon drifted apart. I guess it's hard to love someone else when you don't love yourself. And at the time, I wasn't feeling very good about my life.

Losing a promising job and a serious relationship, practically back to back and both after such a short time, made me melancholy. "If life is one big party," I asked myself, "why do I always feel like I'm on the outside looking in? I'm just having fun and trying not to hurt anyone. So why do I feel so lost?"

I knew other people in the entertainment business had similar feelings, but they did a good job of hiding their emotions. "Everything's great," they always said. Well, if they were great, there must have been something wrong with me because I *never* felt great. I just tried to keep up with everyone around me and maintain a good front.

Not long after the break-up with Valerie, Tommy Morelli, a good friend of mine from Buffalo, asked me to be the best man at his wedding. I agreed. I hadn't been out of California in over a year, so I felt the trip to Buffalo would do me good.

Back to Buffalo . . . Again

I loaded up on supplies of drugs and flew off to party in Buffalo for a week. Tommy picked me up at the airport and drove me to my parents' house.

The first thing my mother said when she opened the door was, "How was the game?"

I stood there staring at her for a moment. Then I remembered that the last time she saw me was when I left Fort Lauderdale to drive to the Super Bowl in January of 1972. I cracked up laughing, and she joined in.

"The game was great," I said. "The Dolphins won!"

Tommy married Paula, a woman we'd both met at the Buffalo Health Spa when I was running Alexander's. We used to go there at four a.m. after work and fall asleep on the lounges by the swimming pool.

About three days after the wedding I was enjoying a meal at a Buffalo café. Michael, one of the café's owners, introduced me to Rob Grill, Warren Entner, and Joel Larson. They were members of the very successful Top 40 rock band called the Grass Roots. The band was in town to play a concert and had stopped into the café for a drink and something to eat.

"We're looking for a manager," Warren said. "Michael told us you have experience in the music business. What are you doing these days?"

"Living at the beach outside LA," I said. "I've been waiting for the right opportunity to come along. Are you offering me a job?"

"Let's talk about it back in California," Warren suggested. "We still have a few more concert dates left on this tour, but we'll be back on the West Coast in a few weeks. Let's get together then." We exchanged telephone numbers.

This sounded like a good opportunity for me, and I was ready to get back to work. I'd been hanging on the fringes of the entertainment business for too long. I had plenty of contacts, but nothing ever turned up that seemed very challenging. Perhaps this would be the next big break for me.

Old Roots, Old Problems

When I got back to California, I called Warren Entner and set up a meeting at his place. He owned a house just above the famed Sunset Boulevard in the Hollywood Hills. It wasn't hard to find.

Warren's maid met me at the door

and told me he would see me in his bedroom. Bedroom? It was three o'clock in the afternoon and he was still in bed? *Hey,* I thought, *this is my kind of guy!*

When I walked into Warren's room, I found him and his wife lying in bed eating clams on the half shell.

Am I dreaming?

I'd thought I was bad, but I might have met my match.

"How's it going?" I asked.

"Listen, Marty," Warren said, moving instantly into business mode, "the band needs someone who knows what he's doing. We haven't really had a hit in a while, but we're still in demand around the country. We want to continue touring and recording while we still have the opportunity. Hopefully, we can come up with another hit record soon."

I told him I was sure I could help.

Warren arranged for me to meet with Rob Grill.

"You're hired," Rob said after I briefly explained my background and qualifications. He made an appointment for me to meet with the band's accountant the next day. Then Rob and I talked for hours and listened to hundreds of records.

Man, I thought again, *this is really living!*

Living. I had no idea what life could

be. I had a lot to learn. But there was still too much in the way for me to learn it. I always overlooked what was important and instead focused on the moment: what looked good, what felt good, what seemed like the things I should want out of life.

I was dead wrong.

> *For the kingdom of God is not meat and drink; but righteousness, and peace, and joy in the Holy Ghost.*
> **(Romans 14:17)**

Chapter 9
Taking the Roots on Tour

I began my first concert tour as manager of the Grass Roots later in 1973. The group consisted of Joel Larson on drums, Reed Kailing on lead guitar, Virgil Webb on organ, Warren Entner on rhythm guitar, and Rob Grill on bass guitar. The whole group also sang, though Warren and Rob handled most of the lead vocals.

My main job was to make arrangements with booking and travel agents, pick up money from the promoters while on tour, and get the group safely from Point A to Point B.

When I interviewed for the job, I made it clear to Rob and Warren that when we were on the road, I would need to be in charge. And I wouldn't allow the band to come near the concert stage until we received payment. They agreed that whenever a problem or situation arose, I would have the final word.

When the day arrived for our first trip out of Los Angeles, I made sure everything was taken care of, including limo service to LAX airport. The night before the flight, I gave the band members three cardinal rules: "We need to always be on time, always look good, and always respect each other's space."

I arranged for everyone to arrive at the airport simultaneously. Rock musicians love to be the center of attention when they travel. They don't like to have the public too close, but when they arrive in an airport, they want people to know they're there. The Grass Roots were no different.

I loved watching the expressions on people's faces when five long, black limos arrived at the airline drop-off point at the same time. They took up the entire curb; no other car could fit. We moved quickly, but still attracted attention. Fortunately, I had also arranged to have a police officer on hand to direct traffic.

"Who are they?" I heard passengers ask. Young girls recognized the band members and ran up to ask for autographs or have their pictures taken with them. We didn't have much spare time, but I had built in a few extra minutes for just this sort of thing. After all, we had to keep the fans happy.

Fly Me—But Not on a Charter

The best way for celebrities to travel was to own their own plane or at least charter one. But several rock stars had gone down in charter plane crashes, including some who had become legendary. Remember Buddy Holly? The Big Bopper? Richie Vallens? Ricky Nelson?

On September 20, 1973, something happened that made us even more nervous about flying charters. Jim Croce crashed and died. The Grass Roots had flown in that same plane and used the same promoter.

The band took Croce's death hard. We used commercial airlines for a while. But the shock from that kind of thing never goes away completely.

Promoters liked to pair bands of equal stature in concerts. The Grass Roots had fourteen Top 40 records, so it wasn't easy for promoters to find bands at their level. And when they didn't, there was always the question, "Who goes on last?"

Of course, the most popular band was supposed to play last, as headliners, with the others as opening acts. Not many of our opening acts had more than one or two hit songs.

But openers liked to upstage the headliners. They were notorious for trying to steal the show. That created a lot of petty jealousy. Of course, pride and ego play a big part in the music business.

We were happy to get booked with bands of equal stature, which included groups such as Three Dog Night and the Beach Boys. When promoters teamed popular bands like that, concert fans certainly got their money's worth. Both groups played nothing but hit songs for the entire set.

When we had three big-name groups on the same bill, the crowd went crazy.

But fame is fleeting. If a successful rock band can't continue making hit records, the quality and size of their concerts decrease. People are no longer interested and the band can't sell enough tickets for big auditoriums in major cities.

The Grass Roots began to see this happening to them. They couldn't come up with another hit record to keep them on top. Their last big hit was *Midnight Confessions*.

Without a stream of hits, life as we knew it ceased to exist. Playing and touring became struggles. The end was in sight.

We had to accept shows in smaller markets. This meant being combined with three or four lesser-known groups and playing for homecomings in small college towns and concerts in remote cities we'd never heard of.

We still partied into the early hours

of the morning, just to stay awake to catch the next day's flight. The band would sleep on the plane and most of the next day at the hotel.

Northern Exposure

In spite of lingering fears, we had to charter small planes to get into some of the small towns. It was a waste of time trying to make connections into small cities. And a charter was more convenient. We had a lot more control over what time we arrived and departed.

One time, the only way we could get to a concert in Billings, Montana, was to charter a small airplane. The pilot picked us up in Denver.

We all had heavy coats with us because it was freezing in Montana. (Actually, freezing would have been a heat wave—It was 15 degrees below zero when we arrived.)

Of course, at the time there were no major car rental companies at the private charter airport in Billings, so I arranged for a local funeral home to rent us a couple of their cars. They pulled up just as we landed.

After the concert, we were invited to a party at what appeared to be the only night-club in town. We arrived to exuberant cheers. Rock stars in Billings!

The women who'd come to the concert hung around the bar with the band. I could tell their boyfriends weren't very happy, watching their girls fall all over us.

Even Pete, one of the roadies, got some extra attention. He loved it. "You're the cute roadie the drummer introduced at the concert," a pretty blonde said, batting her thick lashes at him. "I sure would like to get to know you better."

In spite of the attention, I wasn't thrilled about being at that club. "I don't think this is a good idea," I told Rob. "Something doesn't feel right. Maybe we should all just have one drink and get out of here."

"But there's nothing else to do," Rob said. "If we go back to the hotel, let's at least take a couple of these beautiful women with us."

"Those girls are just teasing their boyfriends," I told him. "There isn't one of them who really wants to party back at the hotel with us. Their boyfriends don't like us, and they outnumber us about five to one."

I watched Pete, the roadie, sitting at the bar, drinking shots of 151-proof rum. He downed ten in the first fifteen minutes. "I'm the band's personal sound engineer," he told the blonde sitting next to him. "If it wasn't for me, they wouldn't sound good at all."

"Oh, that's so exciting," the girl said. "You are so interesting."

The blonde started kissing him and rubbing his neck. Then she looked over at a group of local boys and made a face at them.

"This is my new friend, Pete," she told one of them. "Isn't he cute? And he's with a famous band. Not a loser like you."

That was all the local men needed to hear.

"I'll show you how famous your friend is," one of them yelled as he stormed up to the bar and grabbed Pete by the shirt. He lifted him right off his barstool and threw him onto the floor.

"Let's get out of here," I screamed. "Head for the cars!"

Pete jumped up and we all scrambled out of the bar and into the funeral home cars. As we pulled away, we were pelted with rocks and beer bottles—some of them still full.

The End Comes in Montana?

Just when I thought we'd made it away safely, Pete rolled down the window and started shouting obscenities at the boys from the bar. They chased us all the way back to our hotel.

We managed to make it up to our floor. I called out for everyone to get to their rooms, lock their doors, and stay there until morning.

When morning came, we all met in the hotel restaurant for breakfast. Everyone was accounted for except the pilot. We all figured he'd probably gone to the airport to warm up the plane, load and unload whatever was needed, and make sure it was in good condition to fly. That's what the pilots we'd used in the past all did.

After breakfast, we went out to the cars, only to find them completely destroyed. None of them were even close to drivable. The funeral home was not very happy when I called them to break the bad news about their cars. One month later our accountant received a bill from the funeral home for over seven thousand dollars in damages.

"We'd better get out of here fast," I told the group. "Those boys from last night may still want to try to get us."

I called the local cab company and arranged for two taxis to pick us up and take us to the airfield.

"I hope that plane is ready to go when we get there," I said in the cab. "I don't want to spend another minute in this town."

Not only was the plane still where it was when we first arrived, it was completely frozen, with a thick sheet of ice all around it. And the pilot was nowhere to be found.

Grumbling a few foul words, I called the hotel and rang the pilot's room.

"Hello?" his sleepy voice answered.

"What are you doing in bed?" I bellowed. "We're all at the airport waiting to get out of here. And the sooner the better!"

The pilot, still sounding groggy, apologized repeatedly for oversleeping.

"Listen, buddy," I said, "get out of bed, get dressed as fast as you can, get yourself a big cup of black coffee to go, and get to this airport right away. "

Can We Clear the Trees?

The pilot arrived by cab within fifteen minutes.

Unfortunately, it took him more than two hours to get the plane started. All we could do was sit around and stare at one another. The private charter airport terminal was no more than a shack. It had a coffee machine, an empty vending machine, a rack of old magazines, two chairs, and a rickety wooden coffee table.

Finally, I heard the plane start up. The pilot came running toward the terminal, waving. "All set," he said as he poked his head in. "Let's go."

The band members started tumbling toward the tarmac, but I stopped them at the door. "You just started the plane," I said to the pilot. "Isn't there more you have to do? Like test the flaps or something?"

"No," he said. "The plane's ready."

I grabbed his collar. "You're going to go back out there right now and test those flaps to make sure they're not frozen. After you do that, I want you to take off by yourself a couple of times. Once I see this plane take off and land twice, then and only then will I let the band get on board."

"What, you don't trust me?" he said with an expression of hurt and anger. "I've been flying for more than twenty years, and I've never crashed a plane yet."

"I don't want this to be the first time," I said. "Look, we lost a good friend in a plane crash, and we're all pretty hesitant about flying charter. Even if the rest of the band agreed to get on board with you, I'd stay right here. It's not worth it. Now, if you don't get out there right now, you can consider yourself fired. I'll call another company if you're not out that door in one minute."

He scrambled outside without another word.

When the pilot took off by himself the first time, the airplane barely lifted over the trees at the end of the runway. It veered to the right and almost dove into the ground. He managed to bring the plane around and land, then took off a second time.

His second effort was a little better, but he still came close to the trees on take-off.

"If we were all on that plane the first time, we'd be dead right now," I told the band. "What do you think? Do we want to get on this plane or not?"

We all decided that if the pilot took off a third time and stayed way above the trees, we would go.

When the pilot walked into the airport, I told him to take off again by himself. Without a moment's hesitation, he turned around and did what he was told.

We finally all got in the air and made it safely out of Montana. The pilot didn't say another word the entire flight. We didn't say much either. We just sat there, barely even looking at one another.

Chapter 10
Let the Music Play,
Let the Fun Begin

When I wasn't on the road with the
Grass Roots, I had to live somewhere. So I
decided to rent a house with my friend Gary
Mallaber, former drummer for the Raven. We
found a place with a swimming pool in
Southern California's San Fernando Valley.

Gary was working as a studio musician and often toured with Van Morrison,
Steve Miller, or Paul Williams. But he was
becoming a popular studio musician and
didn't really want to spend a lot of time on
the road.

He got invitations to a lot of sessions, and if I wasn't doing anything at the
time, I tagged along to check out the action.

"John Lennon is in town to record an
album," Gary said one day. "He wants us to
come to the session. Do you want to go?"

"I wouldn't miss it for the world," I told him. "This should be exciting." I hadn't seen Lennon since our heroin balloon episode.

Exciting really wasn't the right word. When we arrived at the recording studio, the place looked like an armed fortress. There were guards everywhere. We walked up to the door and announced ourselves.

"Mallaber and Angelo," the guard said casually as he scanned the list. "OK, I found you. Come right in. It's studio B tonight."

Inside the control room, John greeted us. "I'm trying to get a special sound," he said. "I've invited at least three different musicians for each instrument: guitar, piano, drums, bass guitar, everything."

John didn't choose just any old musicians, either. He picked the most famous professionals he could find. Mick Jagger from the Rolling Stones was in town, so John invited him to join the session. "There must be seventy-five musicians here," I told Gary. "This is incredible."

The drugs flowed freely that evening—like most evenings in the music business. Bags of cocaine lay open all over the control room. People just helped themselves. Not only did they stand there and snort the coke; they also filled their own personal vials.

Lennon had the Record Plant West and A & M Records studios booked for weeks. Word spread fast, and the traffic in front of the recording studios looked like Sunset Strip. Hundreds of photographers set up outside, ready for action. Screaming girls showed up, too, trying to get close to one of their rock star idols.

Sometimes Lennon took hours between songs. Everyone just sat around, got high, and accomplished absolutely nothing. After a few weeks I stopped going to the sessions. "It's not worth it," I told Gary. "It's boring."

Lennon eventually released an album of these sessions entitled: *Rock 'n' Roll*. Phil Spector was the credited producer. History looks at this time in Lennon's life as his fifteen-month "lost weekend" era.

I had a lot of more important, meaningful things to do with the Grass Roots. Traveling with a rock band was far better than sitting around a recording studio doing drugs and not much else.

I was ready to break out, ready to really turn a corner in my life. At least I thought I was. But I didn't have any idea how much further down I would go before I could start to crawl back up.

Back on Tour, Back in Trouble

Life with the Grass Roots wasn't getting any better. We still traveled around the country, taking just about any offer to keep the money flowing.

We played mostly concerts, but from time to time we'd get a call to play a nightclub. A club gig was usually an attractive offer because we could stay in one place for a few days instead of having to travel to do one-nighters. The people at clubs always treated us like stars, and beautiful girls would come from miles around.

We received a terrific offer to play a nightclub in Youngstown, Ohio, near Buffalo. "This one sounds almost too good to be true," our agent told us. "They're paying for everything . . . hotels, airfare, food and drinks, plus they're offering a great fee on top of it."

"Let's do it," Rob Grill said. "After we finish the gig, we can take a few weeks off and relax in Buffalo. Man, I can taste the chicken wings now."

Our agent held a deposit for half of the agreed-upon amount. My first job upon arrival at the club would be to pick up the remainder of the contract fee from the owner, a guy named Freddie. As always, the band would remain in the dressing room until I called them. That way if the promoter didn't have the money ready, the show would not go on. He either had to get the money or cancel the show. Most of the time, the promoters were ready for me. But occasionally, I had to show them I meant business.

Audiences never understand why it takes so long for a concert or a show to begin. They don't realize that a lot of money has to exchange hands at the last minute.

Fifteen minutes before showtime, I walked into the club owner's office at the back of the club and introduced myself. I told Freddie I was there to pick up the rest of our fee.

"Listen, Marty," he said, "we didn't sell too many tickets ahead of time, but we've got a lot of people walking up and buying tickets now. I should have the rest of your money in about an hour."

I gave him the standard answer: "We'll wait."

Freddie didn't look too happy about that, but he didn't argue. He just nodded and left the room.

I sat in the office for a few minutes, admiring the décor. Then suddenly, I heard a Grass Roots song playing. And it wasn't a recording!

What are they doing? I thought. *They know better than to start playing before I have the money in hand. This is crazy.*

It was crazy all right. I just had no idea how crazy it was . . . or how crazy it was about to get.

Just Sing the Songs, Please

The minute the band began to sing, I lost my negotiating power. I was at the mercy of the club owner. Freddie had me! He didn't have to give me another penny. And there was nothing I could do or say.

While I waited for Freddie to get back, I listened as the band continued to play. All I could hear from the office were muffled sounds.

About ten minutes into the show, when they got to the part of their set where the drummer introduces the group, I heard yelling and screaming. I figured the audience must really be enjoying the show.

All of a sudden, a bouncer blasted into the office, with his hands around the neck of one of our roadies, an obnoxious guy named Hank. He was obviously drunk.

"Did you get the money, Marty?" Hank shouted. "Rob wants to know if you got the money."

"Forget the money," I said. "Why is this guy choking you?"

The bouncer opened the closet door, threw Hank in, and padlocked the door.

"What's going on here?" I yelled.

"It seems your roadie likes to get cute," the bouncer said, standing guard at the closet.

"Just tell me what happened," I said with a sigh.

"Get the money," Hank yelled through the locked door.

"Shut up," I hollered back at him.

Just then the club owner came into the room, his face red with rage. "How dare you!" Freddie screamed. "Who do you think you are? I run a respectable place. My whole family is here. The wife and kids are sitting at one of the front-row tables. You have a lot of nerve."

I'd never seen a club owner or promoter this mad. I couldn't hear the band playing anymore.

"Will somebody please tell me what happened?" I asked again.

Freddie pointed a finger at my chest. "When your drummer introduced the band, he also introduced the roadie. When that idiot heard his name, he performed a lurid act right in front of my family!"

"What?" I shrieked. "Are you crazy? Hank would never do anything like that."

The owner came so close I could feel his hot breath on my face. "Are you calling me a liar?"

"Look," I said, trying to restore a

sense of calm to this nightmare, "I'm sorry about what happened. Let's get Rob in here and we'll talk about it with him. He's the owner of the band, the one who signs all the personal appearance contracts."

"I've got your whole group locked in the dressing room," Freddie said, "and I'm not going to let any of them out."

I rolled my eyes. "You can keep everyone else locked up for the time being. Just bring Rob back here."

The owner hesitated, then stormed out of the room, leaving the bouncer still standing guard over the closet.

Freddie returned a few minutes later with three goons. They were dressed in silk suits and looked like mobsters. The two biggest ones dragged Rob between them. He looked as drunk as the roadie. "Did you get the money?" he asked right off.

"Will you stop with the money?" I said, about to lose my cool. "Just tell me what happened with Hank."

"That wasn't really what it seemed," Rob said with a drunken chuckle. "It was just a prop."

The club owner pulled out a 45-cal-iber automatic and pointed it at Rob's face. "Oh yeah? Well, if that was a prop, where is it now?"

Rob shook as if he were about to wet

his pants.

Suddenly, flying out of Billings, Montana, in an ice-covered plane didn't look so risky.

The Buffalo Connection Comes Through

If I had known how to pray, I would have. It didn't look like we were going to get out of that nightclub without getting hurt—or killed.

"Let me make a phone call," I said, trying to think fast. "We're supposed to be in Buffalo tomorrow. You know anyone in Buffalo?"

"Sure," Freddie said. "I know a lot of people in Buffalo."

I rattled off a few key family names I knew. None of them rang a bell. But when I mentioned Carlo Driscetti, my friend Gus's uncle, Fred's expression softened a little. "I know Carlo Driscetti very well," he said.

I asked if I could use his phone to call Carlo. The owner nodded.

When I reached Carlo, I told him what was going on. "I need your help, man," I pleaded. "This Freddie wants to kill us. Can you please talk to him?"

Carlo agreed, and I handed the phone to Freddie.

The club owner gave Carlo his side

of the story, then listened for several minutes. Whatever Carlo said seemed to calm him down. After hanging up, Freddie turned to me and said, "Carlo just got you off the hook, pal." He sat at his desk, pulled open the top drawer, and took out a checkbook and a pen.

"You don't owe us a penny," I said. "In fact, once we get back to Hollywood, I'll ask our agent to send back your deposit."

The group had only played two songs before the roadie broke up the show, so it wasn't worth trying to get paid. It would only add insult to injury.

After giving me a nod of respect, Freddie waved a hand at the bouncer, who let the roadie out of the closet. I gave Hank a glare that told him I didn't want to hear a single word out of his mouth.

We left Youngstown as fast as we could. In the plane on the way to Buffalo, Rob fired Hank, which didn't surprise anyone. Then he dropped a bombshell that sent everyone into shock: "All touring is officially over! I've had it."

After a barrage of noisy arguing, he said quietly, "No more tours. I've thought it over, and I think we all need a break."

I needed more than a break. But I had no clue how to make the break I really needed. I had to be getting close. That, or my game would be over soon. No cat had *that* many lives. Something had to give.

> *For the wages of sin is death; but the gift of God is eternal life through Jesus Christ our Lord.*
> **(Romans 6:23)**

Chapter 11
Somebody Tell Me
What to Do

I was out of control: traveling around the country with famous rock bands, drinking, using drugs, and partying until I was unconscious. Some people might think that sounds like a great life. It wasn't.

I didn't have peace. My heart was empty, just like it was when I was a kid in military school. I still couldn't stand to be alone, so I made sure I was either out all the time or living with someone.

I was searching for something, but I didn't know what. When I traveled by plane, I always stopped in the airport bookstore or newsstand. I combed through whatever books they had, looking for the latest self-help guides or motivational advice to direct my life. I found many spiritual books that looked interesting. But they all seemed to center on someone's interpretation of God mixed in with some special idea they were selling.

I tried just about everything I could to fill what I thought was a void in my life, from Astrology to Zen Buddhism. Transcendental Meditation was hot in the early '70s, especially after George Harrison of the Beatles suggested that everyone try it. I bought every book I could find on the subject. I chanted my made-up mantra for hours on end, but nothing happened. I still felt miserable, lost, and confused.

What is happening to me? I asked myself over and over. *I should be happy. But I'm always depressed and bewildered.*

I couldn't share my discontent with the people around me because they all were just as unhappy as I was—but they didn't admit it or talk about it. I also didn't want to let anyone know I felt so lost. So I put up a good front and appeared to be in control all the time.

The fact that the Grass Roots were still spiraling downward didn't help me personally. But my job allowed me to exist in a state of oblivion. I stayed high on drugs for days at a time. When I sobered up and had to face reality, I saw my life coming to an end. *I can't continue to live like this,* I told myself. But as soon as I said that, I'd get drunk or stoned again. It was a destructive cycle, but I didn't know any other way to live.

> *There is a way which seemeth right*
> *unto a man, but the end thereof are*
> *the ways of death.*
> **(Proverbs 14:12)**

I watched TV when there was nothing else to do. I watched whatever was on, and some of the towns we traveled through didn't have a great selection of channels. I even watched religious shows just to stay awake. It always looked like the people on those programs had some sort of peace inside. But I laughed them off as being foolish or simple-minded. "There is no God," I'd grumble, often out loud. "So who are these people kidding?"

I wasn't sure what I wanted to do anymore. I'd enjoyed traveling and working with the band, but Rob was sticking to his guns about taking a break from touring. I wasn't sure if he'd ever want to get back out on the road again. We met a lot of nice local people and I was thrilled with the other bands we played with. But the descent from the dizzying heights of fame was stressful.

"I guess I'll just hang out here in LA for a while," I said to my housemate, Gary Mallaber. "Just relax, swim in the backyard pool, and party."

But as the Grass Roots began to unravel, something started happening to me. Maybe I was becoming more aware. Maybe I was changing . . . finally.

Then again, maybe not.

I've loved listening to music ever since I was a child. I spent hours in front of my parents' stereo, listening to the latest songs. Whenever I looked back at the important events in my life, I remembered a certain record that was popular at the time. I lived and breathed music. Which is why a career in the music business seemed like such a natural fit.

But my jobs never lasted very long. I couldn't even call what I had a career. It was more like a string of experiences that left me questioning what I was doing and how I would end up.

So, once I had a lot of time on my hands, what did I do? Start to turn my life into something productive? Of course not. I got back into drugging and listening to music.

A Junkie's a Junkie

Not a day went by that I didn't do some kind of drugs. I often stayed awake for days on end, getting drunk and stoned on whatever drug I could get my hands on. But I didn't consider myself addicted. I was just doing what all the other successful people in the music business were doing. Staying high was one of the fringe benefits. Or so I told myself.

Cocaine was the drug of choice in the record industry. It was expensive, but readily available for those who could afford it. Just about everyone I met used it.

Even at business meetings vials of cocaine were passed around for everyone's enjoyment. Some executives had bowls of it sitting on their desks for anyone to indulge in. It almost seemed legal. No one on the higher rungs of the corporate ladder got arrested for it.

I also enjoyed snorting heroin, although I didn't tell my business associates about it. I had some friends who sold it, and they would turn me on for free any time I wanted. I occasionally bought some and got high alone too.

One night, as I was cruising hot nightspots in Hollywood and Beverly Hills, I decided to stop at Ben Franks for a late-night meal. Ben Franks was noted for its famous customers. You never knew whom you would meet there or what might happen.

I was having withdrawal symptoms that night but didn't realize it. The heroin I did before my evening out had worn off and I started having cravings and feeling sick.

I poured half a vial of heroin on the table and proceeded to chop up the drug into two straight lines a few inches long. The restaurant was packed, but no one was paying attention to me.

After I snorted my lines the waitress came for my order. The next thing I knew, I was sitting in the back of a Beverly Hills police car.

"What happened?" I asked the policeman.

"We got a call from your waitress," the cop said. "Seems you passed out at your table." He eyed me suspiciously. "Are you on drugs, sir?"

"No," I lied. "I was only drinking." I was so high I could hardly keep my head up. I kept nodding off and falling over on the backseat. I'd never been higher in my life.

"Let me take a look at your arms, young man," the officer ordered.

I was too high to argue. I rolled up my shirtsleeves and let the cop check my arms.

"No needle marks," he said to his partner.

"We're taking him in anyway," the driver said.

By the time we got to the Beverly Hills jail, I was coherent enough to act offended. "Do I look like a junkie to you?" I asked the booking sergeant.

"What do you think a junkie is supposed to look like?" he shot back. "Look, a junkie is a junkie. And we think you're a junkie."

From Jail to the Brink

Fortunately for me it was so late, the jail didn't have anyone to administer a blood test, so the police just held me in a cell overnight.

I spent the rest of the evening passed out, so I didn't really mind being locked up. When I woke up the next day, I was back to my old demanding self. "What am I doing here?" I yelled out the cell door, adding a small dose of profanity for good measure.

Having announced that I was now conscious, I was set free. No charges were filed.

One of my friends who sold me the heroin picked me up at the station. On the way home Dan told me about a new drug he was experimenting with called STP. "It's kinda like a truth drug," he said. "You take the drug and you get a feeling of truthfulness."

I wasn't very interested in trying that. All I wanted was more heroin. Without it I felt miserably sick.

It took us about three hours to score

the smack. As soon as I snorted some, I felt better. "I can finally think straight," I told my friend.

Dan asked if I was open to trying some STP now.

"Sure, why not?" I said. "I guess it can't hurt."

I didn't feel any immediate effects from the STP, so about an hour later Dan suggested I try some more. The minute I swallowed the next dose, a feeling of exuberance started coming over me. "Great," I grumbled. "I just took a second dose and the first one is finally kicking in."

"Don't worry," my friends assured me. "Everything will be all right." They were either very casual about the experience or they were too stoned to know any better.

All I wanted to do was go home. But my friends were so high they could hardly talk, let alone walk, much less drive.

I called a cab and managed to make it home in one piece. The fresh air made me feel better. I decided to catch up with Rob and some of the boys in the band. They'd told me they were going to the opening of a new club, and I didn't want to miss anything.

I didn't want to miss anything. Now I can see how much of my life revolved around that outlook. There was so much going on and I felt like I had to take it all in.

Obviously, that was impossible, but I had to try. And it almost meant my end.

I took another cab to the club. Shortly after I arrived, a strange feeling of paranoia hit me. I started having hallucinations: quick flashes of light, confused thought patterns, faces of people I knew.

Moments from my past passed before my eyes. That made me really depressed. "My life is a mess," I said over and over. Everything I'd ever said or done flashed before my eyes, and I didn't like one thing I saw.

I gotta get out of here, I thought. *I'm freaking out*.

I took a cab home. When I got there I found a note from Gary saying he was out for the evening.

I went into the bathroom and grabbed a big bottle of Valium. There must have been 500 pills in it. I kept it around because my heart occasionally started beating rapidly. Valium seemed to slow it down. I swallowed three or four pills.

But they didn't help. I just became more depressed.

I turned on the stereo and started listening to a Paul Williams tape Gary had loaned me. The songs Paul was singing hit me hard. They were broken-hearted love songs. The kind only Paul Williams can write. My depression worsened.

"I can't stand this any longer!" I cried out loud. "Life is just not worth living. I want out."

I found some paper and wrote a suicide note. I picked up the bottle of Valium and swallowed all the pills. I gulped them down by the handful.

Then I lay down on the bed, to die. I stared at the suicide note, which I'd dropped on the floor, and kept repeating one line over and over: "I hate life and I hate myself."

A Crazy Ending to a Crazy Time

"How many pills did you take?" someone asked me. "Come on, man. Talk to me. Talk to me!"

I slowly opened my eyes and saw that I was in the back of an ambulance. A paramedic was trying to shove a tube down my throat. "Talk to me," he kept saying. "Talk to me."

I opened my mouth, but I couldn't say a word.

"Speak to me, damn it," he yelled. "Speak to me."

I finally garbled out something.

"The guy is trying to talk," he hollered to the driver. "We need to get his stomach pumped." He turned to me. "What kind of pills did you take?"

130

"Valium," I choked out.

The paramedic finally shoved the large tube down my throat. I vomited a slimy blue liquid all over the place.

Why am I still alive? I thought. *What good am I? I can't even kill myself.*

Shortly after I arrived at the hospital's emergency room, Gary Mallaber came flying in. He looked extremely relieved to see me breathing.

"I came home and found you passed out on your bed. When I read that suicide note, I called 911 right away."

Thanks a lot, I thought.

I had to stay in the hospital for a couple of days for observation before I was released. Then Gary picked me up and drove me home.

When I walked in the door, I found Gary's friend Betty Simmons there. She was a nurse. She said she was going to stay with me for a while.

Betty was friendly and supportive and a good listener. But I was still very depressed.

"I can't even kill myself right," I said over and over.

The next night, when Gary and Betty were watching TV, I remembered another bottle of Valium I had stashed in a cabinet. I snatched it and swallowed the entire contents.

      Betty found me and called 911. Another ambulance came and rushed me back to the hospital. My stomach was pumped again, but this time they held me for psychiatric evaluation.

      "I'm not crazy," I screamed to a doctor.

      But they put me in a mental health ward so they could watch my every move.

      "I am not crazy," I hollered. "You have to believe me."

      But I wasn't sure I believed myself.

Chapter 12
The Dawn of Disco

Following my second attempt at death-by-valium, while I was in the mental ward, Gary called my parents, who were on vacation in Fort Lauderdale, Florida. They flew to LA that evening and were allowed in to see me. My mother was crying when she saw me. My father looked mad.

The doctor decided to release me into their custody. I promised I would get some counseling.

My parents drove me back to my place, where I packed my things and made arrangements to have them shipped to their house in Buffalo. At the age of twenty-nine, I was going back home to live with Mom and Dad.

They didn't want me to stay at my house because they were afraid I'd return to my previous behavior. So I hung out with my folks at their hotel until we could get a flight to Buffalo. It took a couple days to arrange a flight but during that time, I actually started feeling better about myself.

My father was still extremely mad at me, but my mother, as always, was my advocate. "All Martin really needs is someone to tell him 'I love you.' " she said. I knew my mother loved me. My father did too—he just didn't know what to say or how to react to my antics.

Even when my father got mad, which was often, he always supported me in whatever I did. He just saw my life from a different perspective than I did. He didn't understand the music business, and his idea of a job was a lot different from mine.

At the airport waiting for our flight to Buffalo, I bought a copy of *Billboard,* my favorite magazine.

"You ought to read this, Dad," I said, pointing to one of the pages. "This is a very intriguing article on disco music."

He scoffed. "You should just forget about the music business," he said. "Try to find another line of work."

I started to argue with him, but he stopped me with an upheld hand and what looked like moisture in his eyes. "Listen, Martin," he said, "you almost died a few days ago. Why don't you just relax awhile? Once we get to Buffalo, we can get you into some kind of counseling to help you get healthy. Then you can start a new career. A better one. You won't need to worry about disco music or any other kind of music."

Worry? Who was worried? I was interested, curious, and ready to dive into this hot trend and make my mark. From what I'd read, a lot of people were raking in a lot of money at this disco thing. I wanted to be a part of it. Besides, what else was I going to do?

After I settled into my parents' house in Buffalo, I went to a counselor, as agreed. And to a psychiatrist who found me sane. I didn't tell either one about my drug and alcohol abuse because I didn't think it was important. I could control myself. I didn't have an addiction.

At least that's what I believed.

All We Need Now Is a TV Show

New York was where disco started in the US. People loved dancing to it. Unlike rock, pop, or even soul music, dancing to disco music allowed couples to actually touch. The latest craze was the Hustle. I hadn't seen couples touch while they danced since the '50s.

The disco DJ's job was to keep dancers on the floor the whole night. If a DJ failed to keep people dancing, the club owners had the right to fire them. So these guys didn't throw just any old song on the turntable. They practiced for hours on end, testing and trying out different songs.

The nice part of this new era, for me, was that I didn't have to contend with live musicians. I had hundreds of records to choose from, and they didn't say a word! I didn't have to hassle with them when they didn't get out of bed to catch a plane. I didn't have to listen to how much their wives hated one another or how great a performer each considered himself to be. I was in heaven!

Disco records began to outsell all other records in New York. A new era in the music business was born, and I was smack dab in the middle of it.

I knew the disco craze would be a gold mine, but there was still a lot of work to be done. *How can we get more people interested in disco?* I asked myself. The answer shot into my mind like a bullet: a television show. So I decided to start one. I'd never produced a TV program before, but I knew I could do it.

In 1976, at the first *Billboard* Magazine Disco Convention in New York, I met with a small panel of experts. "Disco needs more public exposure," I told them. "A creative television show would get it into people's homes. That way folks can *see* disco."

For the most part, they agreed with me. But no one had tried a disco TV show before. My show would be the first. The ever-popular *American Bandstand* was floundering on pop music, and *Soul Train* had a funky sound that only appealed to a limited audience.

"Disco music needs to become legitimate," I said. "So we need a television program that's as sophisticated as the music. Real disco is refined. It's not bump and grind. All those stringed instruments and horns blend into a fine sweeping and moving sound."

I explained my vision in detail to my friend Eddie Riviera, whose International Disco Record Centre was then a 350-DJ record pool. "I could start it in Buffalo," I suggested. "From there it will spread nationwide."

Eddie shook his head. "Network TV, even at the local level, isn't ready for something unusual like a disco dance show. There's no point in even trying."

Undaunted, I came up another revelation. "Why not try cable television? They'll put on just about anything."

Eddie had no objection to that. So the next day I contacted the local cable provider and made arrangements to launch my new project: a disco TV show. Soon, I would be on the way to fame and fortune . . . again.

I contacted the owner of Club 747, a popular disco club in Buffalo, and told him about my idea. He thought it sounded good and arranged to let me use the club all day on Saturdays. "No one will disturb you," he said. "Even my staff isn't there at that time. But I'll make sure they have the place cleaned up from our Friday night crowd."

After all my searching, all my mistakes, had I finally found my destination? My purpose in life?

I sure hoped so.

Disco Inferno

I named my TV program *Disco Step-by-Step*®. The audience response to our first shows was tremendous. Even though the programs aired in black and white, people still tuned in. Well, people who had cable, of course. I was the show's creator, producer, writer, and its first host.

I spent a lot of time and money letting the folks around Buffalo and the surrounding area know about the program. Word of the show spread like wildfire. It quickly became popular and successful. I was riding the wave of a whole new phenomenon. Finally, everything was truly going my way.

In spite of this most recent success,

my life was still full of confusion and hopelessness. Oh, I seemed happy on the outside. But deep down I was completely empty.

I stayed high almost the entire day, listening to the hundreds of records people sent me. I stayed out all night in bars. It wasn't enough to close a bar at four a.m. I found all the after-hours clubs that featured fast women, gambling, and drugs. Most days I walked out to my car at ten a.m. When other people were already at work for the day, I was just going home.

I was on my way, for sure. But on my way to where? Was I headed in the same direction I'd traveled before? I didn't stop to consider such questions. If I had, I might have been prepared for the problems that were on the way. But some people just can't learn the easy way.

After only a few months on the air, the CBS affiliate for Buffalo called me and said they wanted my show. I was thrilled. I'd approached them with my idea months ago, and they'd laughed at me. "Disco show?" the assistant station manager had said. "No way."

I didn't like some of the conditions of their contract. But I agreed for the sake of the show and my commitment to the disco movement.

This could be my big chance, I thought.

But hold on. I'd had big chances before, hadn't I? The Raven, the Pizza Spot, Alexander's, the Grass Roots. How many big chances would I get?

Stayin' Alive . . . Barely

Disco Step-by-Step® hit number one in its time slot. It even beat out major sports events that aired on other networks.

Every major advertiser wanted to buy time on the show. I laughed when I saw the first McDonald's ad. When I started out, I'd had to beg Visage Hair Salon to buy a $10 spot. Now the largest fast-food chain in the world was buying time.

Disco Step-by-Step® turned out to be the first television show dedicated to disco music, dance instruction, and hustle dancing. It went on to be documented and preserved for future generations by the United States Library of Congress. It also became a part of the Experience Music Project's *Disco: A Decade of Saturday Nights,* featured in the VH1 television documentary *When Disco Ruled the World* and Passport Productions' disco documentary *Disco: Spinning the Story.* Clips of the show were featured on a disco special aired on CBS television's *Sunday Mornings* and was a part of PBS television's *KC and the Sunshine Band Presents: My Music Get Down Tonight - The Disco*

Explosion.

The show's success made my life even crazier. I was no longer hosting my show but had an on-air portion of it, called "Make It or Break It." This was a ten-minute segment in which I presented new releases to the dancers. They would listen to the first minute of each record and yell, "Make it" if they liked the song, or "Break it" if they didn't. I dedicated this segment to Buffalo's granddaddy of rock 'n' roll radio DJs, George "Hound Dog" Lorenz. He first used this idea on some of his early radio broadcasts.

I was usually too drunk or high on drugs to remember much of my segment, but had fun being on camera with the dancers.

During the height of my show's success, my sister, Joanne, started sending me little religious comic-book-type pamphlets known as tracts. One of them was titled, "This Was Your Life." The tract seemed to describe my life perfectly. It showed a man with an obvious drinking problem standing next to a fancy sports car. Because of his superficial success, he thought he had it made. His drinking proved otherwise.

The tract described a "born again" experience. I hadn't heard that expression before. *How can someone be "born again"? I wondered. This is ridiculous. I've heard of far-out people, but my sister must have really gone off the deep end.*

Even though I thought Joanne was losing her grip on reality, I didn't completely disregard the tracts she sent. For some reason, I couldn't bring myself to throw them away, so I tossed them in a drawer. I guess I must have had some respect for religion and didn't want to destroy religious property

My childhood experiences kept me from even thinking about going to church. Every once in a while, though, when I was on the way home from a night of heavy drinking and partying, I stopped at the cemetery to visit my grandmother's grave. But I certainly didn't go there to seek God. I blamed Him for taking my grandma away from me.

It's Fun to Stay at the . . .

I spent most of my days listening to and reviewing albums that record companies sent me. I'd roll a few joints and start my morning with the latest disco hits. Sometimes my review sessions would last through the afternoon. At night, I tested records in discos and nightclubs around the city. I checked out the crowd reaction, identifying which records the audience danced to and noted what songs played before and after. I fed the information to record companies along with personal critiques of the songs. The process took a lot of time but it paid quite well.

London Records national disco promotion man, Billy Smith, picked me among the top twenty most important disco DJs for breaking (introducing) a new disco record. This list appeared in the book *Disco Fever: The Beat, People, Places, Styles, DeeJays, and Groups*. It was written in 1978 by Kitty Hanson and published by Signet Books' New American Library.

In the meantime, Joanne kept sending me religious material. Pretty soon, I felt as if I were on a marketing company's mailing list. I gave the material a quick scan, then tossed it in the drawer. Every tract talked about being "born again." But I still had no idea what that phrase meant.

> *Jesus answered and said unto him, Verily, verily, I say unto thee, Except a man be born again, he cannot see the kingdom of God.* (John 3:3)

One day, Joanne changed her approach. Instead of a pamphlet, she sent me a cassette. In the attached note, she asked me to review the tape and let her know what I thought of it.

Slippery. She knew I couldn't resist reviewing a tape. I was almost proud of her sneaky tactic. She might have made a good music promoter.

So my sister wanted my opinion of a tape? This should be interesting. I threw it into my cassette deck, rolled a couple of joints, lit one, and sat back to listen.

To my surprise, the tape didn't sound at all like a sermon. I was expecting it to be similar to the church services I'd grown up attending, with priests in fancy robes chanting mass in Latin and giving sermons that could have been in Latin, too, for all I cared.

The guy on the tape, Mike Warnke, said he used to be a high priest in Satan's army. That sounded pretty weird. But some of the things he said made sense.

When he claimed that the devil used music to draw people away from God, I almost fell off my chair. According to this man, I was basically working for Satan.

He must be nuts. I've never seen the devil, nor do I receive my paycheck from Satan. This Mike Warnke guy has a lot of nerve.

When he started talking about disco music, I reached over to turn off the tape. But something kept me from hitting the switch. I figured I should listen to what he had to say about the business I was helping to promote.

Warnke said that the entire disco business was a tool of Satan. He quoted a few verses from the Bible about serving the devil instead of God. I had never heard those Scriptures before. The guy went on to describe how disco drew people into an unhealthy lifestyle through music.

In spite of my vehement disagreement with everything Mike Warnke said, I listened to the end. The bottom line to the recording was: "If you don't serve God, you're serving the devil."

> *No man can serve two masters: for either he will hate the one, and love the other; or else he will hold to the one, and despise the other. Ye can not serve God and mamon.* **(Matthew 6:24)**

For weeks afterward, I couldn't get that message out of my mind.

I was sure that I wasn't serving the devil by having a good time. If I wanted to do drugs, whom was I hurting? Myself? Maybe, but that was my choice, right?

> *And if it seem evil unto you to serve the LORD, choose you this day whom ye will serve; whether the gods which your fathers served that were on the other side of the flood, or the gods of the*

Amorites, in whose land ye dwell:
but as for me and my house, we will
serve the LORD.

(Joshua 24:15)

One night, while I was high on the strongest pot I'd ever smoked, the phone rang.

"Hi, Martin," Joanne said. "Did you get a chance to listen to that tape I sent you?"

"Yes," I said.

"What did you think about it?"

"I really don't know what to think."

"How did it make you feel?" she pressed.

"Confused. Angry. If what this guy says is true, I shouldn't even be in the business I'm in. It took me a long time to get where I am, and if I stop now, I'll lose all the momentum I've built. Besides, there really isn't anything else I can do. I live and breathe music, Joanne. It's my entire life."

"Wow," she said. "I never thought you'd react this way."

"Well, I did. So what am I supposed to do now?"

"I don't know," she said. "You're going to have to take that up with God. He loves you and wants to help you."

For God so loved the world, that he

146

gave his only begotten Son, that
whosoever believeth in him should
not perish, but have everlasting life.
(John 3:16)

"Yeah, right," I argued. "God wants to help me? And He loves me? You're nuts."

My sister seemed to be losing touch with reality. She wanted me to talk to God about my reaction to a cassette tape? I wasn't about to take her advice. "Look, I've got to go. I have a ton of work to do. And I would appreciate it if you'd stop sending me this religious nonsense. I'm just not interested."

I slammed the phone down in disgust. *Man, she's got a lot of nerve*, I thought. I was on top of the world, on the verge of making it really big in the music business . . . again. The television show was going strong. I listened to records all day and partied all night. What more could a man ask for?

Chapter 13
The Day the Music Died

Disco Step-by-Step® had a thirty-six-week run on the CBS station. It was everything I had hoped for. But a strange feeling in my gut sensed that something was in the air.

I heard a rumor that the station wanted to syndicate the show. But they wanted to bring in a production company from New York to do the work.

I couldn't believe it. The station wanted to change my show? *My* show? I had already agreed to let someone else host it, but nobody was going to come in and run my show. I owned *Disco Step-by-Step*®. I'd created it. I wrote it. I dreamed it. It was all I had. Losing it would destroy me.

Without even consulting me, the station made a deal with a production company from New York City to take over the show. They offered me a job as assistant producer.

I felt like somebody had shot an arrow into my heart. My mind filled with rage. I was almost too angry to speak.

"It's just business," they told me. They also said they would move ahead with or without me. They could change the name of the show if they had to. I was either in on their terms or out of the picture completely.

I chose out.

Deciding I needed a break from Buffalo, I drove to Miami. My friends Gus and Chick Driscetti had moved there, and they'd told me I was always welcome to come by any time.

Good-bye, Buffalo; Hello, Sunshine

Three years or so before, my father had retired and my parents moved to Fort Lauderdale. So I stopped by to see them on my way to visit Gus and Chick. They were glad to see me, but they could tell I was depressed. My mother told me I should pray to Jesus for help.

"Oh, no," I grumbled. "Not you too. I'm out of here!" I left for Gus and Chick's, cutting off my mother's lecture.

"My mom and my sister actually talk like they know God personally," I told Gus. "I think they're losing it. They've turned into Jesus freaks."

Life at Gus and Chick's house seemed just like the good old days. They had a beautiful house in Coconut Grove, a condo on Key Biscayne, and another house on Hibiscus Island, made famous by the notorious mobster Al Capone. Whatever they were doing for a living must have been sweet.

"I've been put through the ringer," I said to Gus after telling him about the TV show fiasco. "I can't believe this. Just when I was on the verge of making it, this had to happen. I'm not sure I can take it anymore."

Gus invited me to live in one of their houses. "There's plenty of room here," he said. "And Florida has everything: wine, women, and song."

I decided to stay.

Gus was living with his girlfriend at his Key Biscayne condo, so I moved in with Chick at the house on Hibiscus Island. The two of us got along well together. We both liked to drink and do drugs. We sat around for hours just getting high.

But I had a rough time trying to break away from my work. Eddie Rivera still called me constantly to ask what I thought of a certain record. I received hundreds of demo records from companies I represented. But I soon lost interest in disco and only listened to a few records each day.

I had a complete disco sound system in my bedroom and spent a lot of time mixing records between turntables. Of course, I snorted a few lines of cocaine between records.

"I need to put things into perspective," I said to Chick. "I think I'll take a trip out to California to see Mike Goldstein. He's been in the music business longer than I have. Maybe he has some ideas for me."

California and Cocaine

Mike and I had become close when I first lived in LA and I was working with the Grass Roots. We'd remained friends ever since.

He loved the music business as much as I did except that he wasn't into disco. He promoted various rock groups and mainly worked independently. He had jobs with major record companies, but Mike worked best alone. He was an old radio promoter and he knew his business well. He knew what the stations wanted and would only represent hit records. "No stiffs," Mike insisted. "I do not promote stiffs."

The one thing Mike and I had in common besides our love for the music business was our love for cocaine. He always had the best and was willing to share it with anyone around him. A day didn't go by that Mike didn't grind up a few grams, whether he was in the office or out on the road. Whenever Mike came into town, everyone knew that the best cocaine for miles around had arrived.

And Mike always took care of his friends. "My coke is your coke," was one of his favorite expressions.

Although Mike gave away a lot of cocaine, he also had a list of people who insisted on buying it from him. "You can only give so much away," he said. "Some of these people want their own stash, and who am I to refuse? Besides, I need some of them to help me with my business."

"You don't have to make any excuses to me," I told him. "You're selling it to your friends. That's not dealing. It's not like you're out on the street selling it to kids or anything. Those are the guys who should be locked up."

It seemed everyone associated with the music business consumed drugs. But safety in numbers didn't make what we did legal. Deep down, I knew selling drugs to friends was illegal. I just didn't stay straight long enough to think about it.

After a month, I decided to go back to Miami. I'd had enough of the Hollywood scene and wanted to relax in the Florida sun.

Life in Florida had gone on without me while I was gone. The partying had increased and the drugs flowed even more freely than before. "It seems like you have an unlimited supply," I told Chick. "I've never seen us go through so much before, and you haven't asked me for a dime. Are you into something I don't know about?"

He never admitted to selling drugs. But I knew there was no other way he could live the kind of life he was living.

The Definition of a Drug Dealer

After a month of relaxing in Florida, I decided to go back to California, this time to see if I could find any music business jobs.

I knew Mike went through a lot of drugs out in California, and Chick seemed to have more than he needed. So I asked him if I could take a few ounces with me. He readily agreed, and I stuffed the coke into my briefcase. (Airport security was a lot looser back then.)

When I showed Mike the cocaine I'd brought with me, he was impressed. Next thing I knew, Mike was on the phone with his dealer, a retired actor named Benny.

When I walked through his front door with Mike, Benny was sitting on the couch watching television. He asked what we had to show him. I pulled out the cocaine I'd brought with me from Florida.

"This stuff looks pretty good," Benny said, examining it. "I'll take all you've got."

I told him I had four ounces. He paid

$1,500 per ounce, a total of $6,000. Chick had only paid around $1,000 for it. I'd just made a $5,000 profit! And Bennie said he would take as much of the stuff as I could get him.

"That was easy," I told Mike as we drove back to his house.

I flew back to Florida, proud of my latest endeavor. When I handed Chick the $6,000 and told him that Benny wanted more, Chick was delighted.

I still didn't consider myself a drug dealer. I figured since Benny was a friend of Mike's and Mike was a friend of mine, that made it OK. Just a casual transaction among friends.

I didn't want to tell Benny that he was my only customer. He thought he was working with a big-time dealer. I didn't bother correcting his misperception.

Not long after that visit to California, I was relaxing in my south Florida home one sunny day when suddenly the place was surrounded by twenty-five police officers with their guns drawn.

"The party's over," one of them yelled. "Get your hands up. You're under arrest for possession of cocaine and conspiracy to distribute."

Chapter 14
At Last, the Big Deal Happens

We've finally caught up to where I started. Remember Chapter 1? The big south Florida drug bust in the summer of 1980. The scene out of *Miami Vice* before there was a *Miami Vice*.

I'd been busted, and I knew I could go to prison for a long time if I couldn't find some way to worm my way out of it, get off without paying any harsh penalty. I just wanted to get back to my life so I could start searching again for my next big break.

My parents put up their house as collateral to pay my bail. After I got out, the partying continued. I still did drugs, not believing anything bad would happen. After all, I'd gotten out of plenty of other situations, raised myself up from all those problems. Why would this time be any different?

A Funny Thing Happened on My Way to Die

While waiting for the outcome of a grand jury investigation, I decided to travel to Buffalo to see some friends. But none of them wanted to see me. What a kick.

Out of friends, out of a job, and out of money, I was losing my identity. Marty the cool band manager, Marty the TV show pioneer, even Marty the partier, were all gone. I had nothing left to boast about. No big deals, no fame, and definitely no fortune.

Nine months after my arrest, I checked myself into the New London Inn, a fleabag shack. I figured it would be as good a place as any to die. I called my sister to let her know where I was.

I was at rock bottom. I had been close to this before. But when I had messed up in the past, I at least had a little bit of rope left, something to grab on to and use to pull myself back up. This time, I had nothing going for me. No bands to manage, no bars to tend, no TV shows or star treatment for me. I had a good taste of the empty life that I'd seen everyone else living.

I had nothing left to boast about. No ego, no job, no credentials, and no identity beyond a name that no one seemed to want to hear anymore. Maybe I was a drug dealer after all. That was the only identity that seemed to stick to me.

After a few days in the New London Inn, I lay down on the bed, completely empty of any emotion, just hoping, somehow, that death would knock on the door and take me away.

Instead, the phone rang. My sister, Joanne, called to ask me to come stay with her. She told me she loved me—something she had never said before. She started to cry. I told her I would drive out to see her.

Before that moment I would have hung up on her. But after thirty-five years of messing up, I had finally reached bottom. I didn't have anywhere else to go. Death hadn't even had the decency to find me at the New London Inn. So I drove to Joanne's.

Something was happening to me that I couldn't explain. I wasn't even really aware of it at the time. I know now that the Scripture seeds Joanne had been planting were beginning to take root. Those annoying pamphlets, tracts, and cassette tapes were the seeds. They were what got me to look at myself, examining what I really saw in the mirror.

When I got to Joanne's, I told her I wanted what she has. "But it has to be right now," I demanded in desperation. She said she wanted to try something unusual that she said would help me. I wasn't very excited

about any freaky do-it-yourself religious cer-
emonies, but I agreed to go along with
Joanne's idea. After all, what did I have to
lose?

Now, That's Show Business

My sister called some friends of hers
and we drove over to see them. They lived in
a converted farmhouse in Springville, New
York. One of her friends, Rudy Cegielski,
was a minister. He and his wife, Marie, met
us at the farmhouse. They and a small group
of others stood around me in a tight little cir-
cle. They read from the Bible and prayed.
They said they were going to "lay hands" on
me and that I should expect something to
happen. They said that God was going to
work a miracle in my life.

Rudy asked me if I wanted to be
"born again." I remembered those words
from Joanne's gospel tracts.

> ***Jesus answered and said unto him,***
> ***Verily, verily, I say unto thee, Except***
> ***a man be born again, he cannot see***
> ***the kingdom of God.*** **(John 3:3)**

Yeah, I thought. *I would love to be*
born all over again. To have a new chance at
life. I've tried everything else, and nothing
seems to work. I'm ready to try whatever

160

God has for me. "Yes," I said. "I do want to be born again."

Rudy asked me if I thought I was a sinner.

> **For all have sinned and come short of the glory of God.**
>> **(Romans 3:23)**

"I sure am," I said. "No doubt about it."

He asked if I believed that Jesus had come to earth, died, and rose from the dead.

> **That if thou shalt confess with thy mouth the Lord Jesus, and shalt believe in thine heart that God hath raised him from the dead, thou shalt be saved.**
>> **(Romans 10:9-10)**

"Of course," I answered.

He asked if I was willing to repent, to turn from my sins and sinful ways.

> **Then Peter said unto them, Repent, and be baptized every one of you in the name of Jesus Christ for the remission of sins, and ye shall receive the gift of the Holy Ghost.**
>> **(Acts 2:38)**

161

"For sure," I responded, choking back emotions that seemed to clog my throat.

Rudy instructed me to ask God to forgive my sins and to come into my life.

> *If we confess our sins, he is faithful and just to forgive us our sins, and to cleanse us from all unrighteousness.* **(John 1:9)**

I did so, quickly and willingly.

The group around me then laid their hands on me. At that precise moment, I heard three loud claps of thunder—*boom, boom, boom*—all in a row.

I felt something surging inside me. It felt like an electrical current was racing through me. I started to speak in another language (a phenomenon later explained to me as the baptism of the Holy Ghost with the evidence of "speaking in tongues"). I felt on fire and excited. I felt as if either lightning had hit me or I'd jammed a finger into an electrical outlet.

You might say I was in my own electric chair. But instead of dying as a punishment, my old life died. And I was given a new one.

The sensation lasted for only an instant. But at that moment, I experienced a high that nothing could match—not booze, drugs, or even making love. I felt a sense of calm, a peace. And suddenly, everything made sense. Everything that had happened in my life to that point finally made sense to me.

> *If the Son therefore shall make you free, ye shall be free indeed.*
> **(John 8:36)**

I felt as if a warm shower hit me all at once. Actually, it was more like a waterfall. There wasn't any physical sensation of getting wet; just a complete immersion in that sense of peace, like I was floating and no longer weighed down.

Not everyone experiences such an amazing conversion when they accept Jesus Christ as their Savior. But God knew I needed something dramatic. I'd been in show business my entire life. I can just imagine God saying, "You want show business? I'll give you some show business!"

I haven't been the same since that day. Once I got a taste of God, I couldn't go back to my old life.

They say that before you die, your life passes before your eyes. You get to see a little film of everything you've done up to that point. Good and bad. I didn't die physically, but I did die on the inside. And I don't know if I saw my whole life on film, but I finally understood. I thought about the things I'd done and I saw how meaningless they were, how ridiculous I was to chase money, fame, and the highs I got from drugs and booze.

I had finally found what I was unknowingly searching for most of my life: the kingdom of God.

> *But seek ye first the kingdom of God, and his righteousness; and all these things shall be added unto you.* **(Matthew 6:33)**

> *...who hath delivered us from the power of darkness, and hath translated us into the kingdom of his dear Son.* **(Colossians 1:13)**

It's funny how two paths to two completely different destinations can exist almost side by side, but they do. At many places in your life, you have a choice to go in one direction or the other. That night at Joanne's friend's house, I finally made the right decision, the choice to go in the right direction.

My life changed that night, and it's a change that will last forever—literally, because I can experience God's kingdom here on earth now, and I have life after death for all eternity.

For the kingdom of God is not meat and drink; but righteousness, and peace, and joy in the Holy Ghost.
(Romans 14:17)

I moved into Joanne's house after my conversion. I didn't feel the least bit uncomfortable being around her spiritual outlook on life. The only thing I was uncomfortable with was the still-looming prospect of trial and prison for my south Florida drug-dealing arrest. I prayed for God's will to be done in that situation.

I started to attend church at the Full Gospel Tabernacle in Orchard Park, New York. The pastor, Tommy Reid, helped me get grounded in God's Word. I was later baptized in water in the name of Jesus Christ for the remission of my sins. I was actually following God's plan of salvation according to what Jesus' apostles taught after He rose from the dead and poured out His Holy Spirit on them on the Day of Pentecost.

Then Peter said unto them, Repent, and be baptized every one of you in the name of Jesus Christ for the remission of sins, and ye shall receive the gift of the Holy Ghost.
(Acts 2:38)

I wasn't following any denominational mandates or doctrines. Just doing what the Bible clearly stated. I didn't accept Jesus into my life in a church but in an old converted farmhouse outside Buffalo, New York. God is not a respecter of buildings. He will move wherever you are in your time of need.

I hired a lawyer in Buffalo. He eventually found out that I was going to be indicted. My life, though radically changed in the conversion, went from scary to surreal. It was the sort of thing you might expect to see in a movie.

My rapid heartbeat returned, and I had to be hospitalized. But the criminal justice system waits for no man, sick or healthy. A federal judge from Buffalo came to the hospital to deliver the indictment. The judge, a prosecutor, my attorney, a federal marshal, and the court reporter all gathered in my hospital room for an official hearing.

Where God Wanted Me

After I was indicted, I went back to Florida to get ready for my court hearing. I decided to plead guilty to the charges, knowing I *was* guilty and wanting to get my old life behind me. No matter what my fate would be, I was content.

I began attending church, spoke to youth groups about the perils of drug use,

166

and participated in meetings sponsored by the Full Gospel Business Men. The support I felt from the people there was amazing.

Sometimes I wondered if the men who gathered there really knew who I was. But at least one guy did. The most important man I would meet at those meetings was a police officer, Detective Frank Rossi. As soon as I met him, I explained who I was and what I was up against. As we got to know each other at the meetings, we became friends. Detective Rossi could see that I hadn't been saved just out of convenience, in the hope that it would get me a lesser sentence.

I asked the detective what I could expect in the sentencing part of the trial.

"You're a new man," Rossi said. "Don't worry about that old stuff."

I looked into alternative sentencing options, programs that could mean no prison time. I wanted to live at the Bridge, a residential program run by ex-convict Frank Costantino of Christian Prison Ministries of Orlando, Florida. He'd written a book called *Holes in Time*, which I had read while in Buffalo. He had a tremendous ministry to prisoners and ex-prisoners, and I wanted to be part of it.

Detective Rossi asked me if I wanted him to speak on my behalf at my sentencing.

I told him he didn't have to do that. In fact, my lawyer didn't want Rossi to say anything. Instead, he told me to have Rossi write a letter for me. I didn't understand why. But that was part of the plan as we went to the courthouse for the sentencing.

When the pivotal moment came, the judge asked, "All right, anybody else have anything to say?"

At that point, Detective Rossi stood. The judge acknowledged him by name without being introduced. Apparently they knew each other.

In spite of what my lawyer had said, Detective Rossi told the judge how I had changed. He described what I'd been doing: speaking to young people, going to the gospel meetings, and talking about faith in Jesus Christ. He said he was convinced that I was sincere in my conversion, that I was truly a changed man thanks to being born again on that electrifying evening at my sister's friends' house.

At that point I sensed that everything was going to come out all right. I knew God wanted me to do something important with my life, to tell people how I had messed up for so many years, but that He was watching over me and had rescued me when my life seemed over. So I knew that whatever happened in the next few minutes would be a part of that plan.

"Well, Mr. Angelo," the judge said, "I hope what Detective Rossi testified is right and you have changed. Because I'm going to put you where you're needed most. I'm sentencing you to two consecutive three-year terms in the Federal Correctional Institution in Lexington, Kentucky."

"Wow! Praise the Lord," I said to myself, "I can finally begin my new life in Christ."

I wasn't getting off with community service or probation. I wasn't going to be rewarded for my conversion. No evangelizing for God to repay His intervention. No freedom. I was going off to prison as a changed man filled with the Holy Ghost. I wondered how much time the judge would have given if Detective Rossi didn't testify on my behalf.

I thanked God for allowing me to be sentenced to six years in prison. I knew in my heart that my sentence was God's will. The hand of God was in this. He had used the judge to do His will, and He was going to work through me too.

I finally knew where I was going. And I knew it was where God wanted me to be. I'd wanted to go to Bible college. Maybe in prison I could take correspondence courses.

When I got to prison, I didn't want to waste one second of my time. I had devoted my life to God. No matter where I was, I was going to serve Him.

I was finally beginning to understand.

> *Therefore if any man be in Christ, he is a new creature: old things are passed away; behold, all things are become new.*
>
> **(2 Corinthians 5:17)**

Chapter 15
Inside the Big House

In January 1982, I walked into the Federal Correctional Institution in Lexington, Kentucky. As a Christian, it almost didn't matter that I was going into prison. I was determined to tell everyone there about the amazing conversion I had experienced. And I would tell them that if it can happen to someone like me, after all the trouble I'd caused in my life, it can happen to anyone, even convicts.

I wanted to start reaching out right away. I had a suitcase full of Christian books and tracts like the ones Joanne had sent me. According to the prison rules, an inmate is allowed to bring in some clothes, shoes, a Bible, a few books, and a couple of photographs. A suitcase full of tracts, books, and Bibles was really pushing the limits. But I didn't know that at that time.

When the prison guard who inspected

my belongings saw the suitcase overflowing with religious goodies, she stepped back and looked me up and down. "I can't wait to read your file," she said. "What did you do, rob your church's poor box?" She thought I was a church leader gone astray.

I sensed she was a Christian because she let me take in the entire suitcase.

I started spreading the material around the prison. I gave tracts to cons who said they were Christians but didn't really care about God, to guys who had no faith, even to Muslims and to Jewish inmates, who turned out to be my greatest challenge.

I met a couple of Jewish inmates in my housing unit. One of them, Nat, suggested I pass out my tracts to the other Jewish prisoners. He invited me to one of their community meetings and told me I should speak to the people there. He even advised me to tell the rabbi about Jesus.

I thought this would be a great opportunity to evangelize because they usually drew about seventy inmates to their meetings. After my conversion, I had attended Temple Aaron Kodesh in Fort Lauderdale, which was a church for Messianic Jews. (That's someone who is born Jewish, wants to remain Jewish, but considers himself a *completed Jew* because he believes that Jesus is the Messiah, the Son of God.) At Temple

Aaron Kodesh, I went forward when the pastor issued an altar call. He said there were people at the service whom God was calling to be ordained evangelists or ministers to Jewish people. When I heard that, I ran down to the altar. So I felt I had a place in attending the Jewish inmates' meeting.

When the meeting began, Nat didn't introduce me as Jewish, but as a "Jew for Jesus."

Two inmates immediately got up and left. The rabbi looked at mc and shook his head. Everyone else started chuckling.

My friend had set me up. It was a joke. The Jewish inmates didn't want to hear about Jesus. A lot of the guys there didn't even care about Judaism; they just wanted to get into the kosher kitchen because the food was much better than what was served to the prison's general population.

The prison chaplain, Rev. Warren Schave, pulled me out of the meeting. He sat me down for a little chat, drawing a diagram on a slip of paper to help explain the law of prison religious services.

"There are Catholics, Protestants, Muslims, and Jewish inmates in here," Rev. Schave said, pointing to his quickly drawn four-box diagram. "My job is to make sure that everyone gets the services they need, not to try to convert anyone." He suggested I not disrupt the Jewish meetings by talking about Jesus. He didn't know I had already spread many "Jews for Jesus" tracts around the prison.

One day the head of the Jewish congregation, a massive guy named Stanley, approached me with a baseball bat in his hand. He said he was going to club me to death for leaving "Jews for Jesus" tracts in their minutes-of-the-meeting books stored in the chaplain's office.

One of the other inmates quickly notified a guard, and he stopped Stanley from following through on his threat. The guard then sent two other guards to my cell and confiscated all the religious materials out of my locker: every book, tract, and Bible.

Some time later, Stanley tried to escape. After he was captured and brought back to the prison, the only people who would talk to him were me and a few of the other Christian inmates. That really struck home with him. About three weeks later Stanley accepted Jesus Christ into his life and was born again. Praise the Lord!

After his conversion, he started praising Jesus all the time and reaching out to the rest of the Jewish inmates. Many others came to know Christ through Stanley's ministry.

In This Corner . . .

The first lesson in picking fights is to go after someone you know you can beat. I don't remember having too many fights in my life. Then again, I don't remember if I ever thought there was much worth fighting over.

So it was a little surprising in late 1982, nearly a year after landing in Lexington, to find that I was headed for a fight. I didn't pick this one—not intentionally, anyway. I would never have started a fight with a guy who had been one of Muhammad Ali's sparring partners.

One of the jobs I held in the prison was in the hospital ward's physical therapy department. Ali's sparring partner, Willie Brown, hurt his back working out in the yard and came in to see the physical therapist for treatment. During his treatment, he was under orders not to work out. But he did anyway.

The physical therapist found out. I don't know how she knew. But for some reason Willie thought I'd ratted him out.

He swore he would get me. He knew where I spent time in the prison yard each day. I always hung around with the Christian inmates. Every day for the next couple of weeks, whenever Willie saw me in the yard, he would yell at the top of his lungs,

"Angelo, I'm gonna beat you!"

The whole yard heard him yell at me each time.

One day, armed with more faith and conviction than smarts or muscle, I confronted Willie. "Before you can beat me," I said, "you're going to have to get my father's permission."

"Oh, yeah?" he answered. "Who's your father? Is he in here too?"

I told him Jesus Christ was my father.

I thought he'd be stunned or at least a little shocked to hear me say that out of the blue. But he wasn't.

"You know, I consider Jesus Christ to be my father too," Willie said calmly. "And if Jesus is your father and He's my father, that makes us brothers, so we shouldn't be acting this way."

I stood there amazed. In prison, whenever someone says the words *Jesus Christ*, except as a swear phrase, most cons will say, "Get away from me." If inmates know you're a devout Christian and you sit down at a dining hall table, most will get up and sit somewhere else. It makes it hard to evangelize, but it can also be a form of protection.

Yet in this situation with Muhammad Ali's sparring partner, Jesus Christ had protected me in a way I would never have imagined.

Willie later recommitted his life to Jesus and came to many of our fellowship meetings. He said he didn't care what the rest of his old friends had to say about his return to Christ. He told me Jesus set him free and he was proud of it. He didn't mind being seen with Christians. We even jogged together many times. What a sight! We looked like David and Goliath running around the yard.

Overcoming Fear

For Christians and non-Christians alike, prison can be the most frightening place to be. No freedom; only a dull, robot-like existence every day. That's enough to drive anyone to violence.

When you're on the outside, thinking about the prospect of going into prison, it's a scary thought. Just the word *prison* can create tough images.

The Lexington Correctional Institution wasn't maximum security, but it had all levels of inmates because it was one of only two prisons in the federal system that had a hospital. So you never knew what kind of criminal you were going to run into in the course of your day.

But the prison itself didn't really frighten me. Like in most situations, the greatest fear is of the unknown. I learned from the Bible:

> *"For God hath not given us the spirit of fear; but of power, and of love, and of a sound mind."*
> **(2 Timothy 1:7)**

This was one of the most important Scriptures I ever memorized.

Fortunately, Jesus Christ knows everything, so we can trust in Him, no matter how scary our circumstances. For Christians, the only time we fear is when we separate ourselves from Him.

Overcoming Boredom

I had a lot of time to think in prison. After all, there were few distractions there. I was determined to make the most of my time. So I took correspondence courses from four different Bible colleges: Vision College, Berean College, Full Gospel Bible Institute, and Rhema Bible College.

Many prisoners don't do much while they're incarcerated. They just serve their time. They're not really interested in improving themselves. I, on the other hand, never felt like I had enough time to do all the things I wanted to do. I let time serve me, instead of just sitting there serving time.

178

If I'd let myself focus on the fact that I had no physical freedom, no say in what I did or where I went each day, I would have been a mess. And I saw a lot of inmates who let themselves get that way. But because I had goals and a reason to get up off my bunk each morning, prison didn't feel like such a horrible place. The iron bars and stone walls were constant reminders that I wasn't going anywhere, but I dealt with them by keeping myself busy.

After about two and a half years in prison, I had graduated from all four Bible colleges and earned ministerial degrees from them, becoming a licensed minister. I also completed every self-help program the prison had to offer, from Transactional Analysis to Zig Zigglar's Positive Mental Attitude courses. I never let a second slip by unused because I knew I would never have this amount of free time on my hands again.

Overcoming Sin

Most people who've never gone to prison probably figure it's the lowest point in anyone's life. I guess that's why everyone thinks just one trip to prison should straighten out every criminal. Just put them in a place that no one would ever want to go and they'll realize how much better they had it outside. Then they'll get their lives together and become productive, responsible members of society.

But that's not what usually happens. When I was in prison, I witnessed many different strange behaviors. One in particular was inmates sneaking food and sugar out of the prison mess hall. Seems innocent enough, huh? Just food and sugar. But those inmates would get caught for breaking the prison's rules, which got many of them more time in prison, which delayed their parole. Some were even shipped off to a higher-level prison. For food and sugar! Now, if prison life hadn't stopped those inmates from breaking simple rules, what would?

Only one thing can truly change a person's life. And that's a personal relationship with the living God, our Lord and Savior, Jesus Christ.

Unfortunately, a lot of people have to hit rock bottom before they'll even consider Jesus. And for a lot of folks, prison is the bottom.

Prison did have the worst living conditions I've ever known. But I had hit bottom before I went in.

If I hadn't found the bottom of human existence before prison, would I have ever found it? Probably not. Most likely I would have wound up doing something that got myself even deeper in trouble. I could have also died in my sins.

I might have made it through prison without my conversion, but I think God understood what I needed. He'd seen how lost I was—and He knew what had to happen to get me on the right road. Going to prison helped me and turned out to be a real blessing instead of a curse.

But that's my story. I don't know what it takes for somebody else. That's between each individual and God. I know Jesus is real and is a way maker. And He will make a way for anyone willing to follow Him.

You might not experience exactly what I did. Because salvation is personal. And Jesus is a personal God. He meets you wherever you are. All you have to do is open yourself up to Him.

> *Behold, I stand at the door, and knock: if any man hear my voice, and open the door, I will come in to him, and will sup with him, and he with me.*
>
> **(Revelation 3:20)**

Once He does move in your life, you'll know. And you'll know it beyond a shadow of doubt.

Freedom

I don't remember the day I got released on parole in 1984 as a particularly important moment. But I do remember the life lessons I learned while I was there. The most important thing I learned was that the kingdom of God is *now* within me. There is no need to wait until the "sweet by-and-by." I can have everything Jesus has for me right now.

> *Neither shall they say, Lo here! or, lo there! for, behold, the kingdom of God is within you.*
> **(Luke 17:21)**

> *For the kingdom of God is not meat and drink; but righteousness, and peace, and joy in the Holy Ghost.*
> **(Romans 14:17)**

Those statements are easier to say than to explain. But all that I went through before I was arrested—living an empty life of drugs and booze, getting arrested, waiting for the indictment and sentencing, and then the most important moment in my life when I was saved—taught me that God is always with us, waiting for us to exercise the free will to choose Him.

If there's one thing that I want people who read my story to understand, it's that

Jesus Christ is always ready for us to ask Him to come into our lives and be our Lord and Savior. He loves us so much and will give us the desires of our hearts if we will just put our trust in Him.

Chapter 16
Between Songs

Now that I've been out of prison for more than twenty years, life is great . . . but not perfect. That might be one of the biggest mistakes any ex-con makes, thinking life will be ideal once they're out. You have freedom again, and that is a tremendous blessing. But it also carries an enormous responsibility: living within the boundaries of the law.

Since I became a Christian in 1981, I've never felt like I was alone. Jesus has always been there to pick me up when I was down and shower me with His love and grace.

So, when I need a little support, I know exactly where to go. "OK," I say to Jesus, "what's the next step You want me to take?" It's an open dialogue between God and me.

When I remember the heartache of my old life, it's easy now to see that God's hand was leading me, guiding me, even though I didn't know it at the time. Jesus Christ still leads me . . . only now, I follow.

Life on the Farm—No Green Acres

If I ever give in to pride and think that I've accomplished so much and done such a good job of turning my life around, I know I'm not on the right path. No matter how much I've achieved, no matter how much you achieve in turning your life around, there's always plenty more to do.

"God's not finished with us yet."

Those words are from Rev. Garland "Pappy" Eastham. I met Pappy after I got out of Lexington in 1984. I was living in a Fort Lauderdale halfway house run by the Salvation Army, and the counselor there suggested I check out a place named Faith Farm.

"A farm?" I asked. "What do they do there, pick beans?"

The counselor told me it was a church that feeds, houses, clothes, and disciples more than 350 alcoholics and drug addicts each day. He made arrangements for me to meet the founder, Rev. Eastham.

We met at a Denny's restaurant for breakfast. I expected to see a conventional minister in a nice pressed suit. But what I saw walking toward me was an old man covered with dirt. He had just finished demolishing a cinder block wall and jumped into his car to hurry over to meet me without even changing clothes.

"God sent you to me, my son," Pappy said as soon as he saw me.

Like every other ex-con on parole, I had to hold down a job. When I first got out of prison, my cousin had given me a job selling timeshare units for a local condo complex. It wasn't exciting, but it was a job. And it allowed me to attend Pappy's daily morning Bible study at Faith Farm.

I soon quit the timeshare job and went to work full time at Faith Farm as a live-in employee, in charge of selling thrift store furniture. It was the best place I could have spent that first year after prison. I was getting truly grounded in the Word by attending daily Bible studies and church services three times a week. I also spent countless nights sitting with Pappy studying the Bible and analyzing his array of Bible-related charts he designed on window shades. That was a precious time for me.

Pappy Eastham might have seemed like a crusty old guy, looking more like a field worker than a minister. But what he lacked in appearance, he more than made up for with faith. The field he tended, his form of ministry, was the field of troubled souls.

Any addict, alcoholic, or homeless person down on his luck was welcomed to Faith Farm. And Pappy made sure they had plenty of work to keep their minds off their troubles.

Pappy was a character, but a man who lived the way Christians are supposed to live. He definitely walked the walk. Rough around the edges, and the first to admit it, Pappy wanted to set an example every day. It didn't matter that he wasn't refined or eloquent. It didn't matter to him that he had few resources. "You don't give up and stop what you're doing," he'd say. "Once you know the truth, where are you going to go?"

Faith Farm Ministries has gone where the Lord wants it to go. From that one location in Fort Lauderdale, it has grown. Now, there are two more locations: Boynton Beach and Okeechobee. I'm proud to have been a part of what Faith Farm has become.

New Challenges

In 1985, after a year with Faith Farm, God opened a door for me to work as a live-in counselor with a ministry called Teen Challenge of Southern California. I ministered there as a counselor less than a year, which helped establish a pattern that continues today. I believe God calls each of us to do specific things in our lives and that He has a plan for us. And I'm on the road He wants me to walk, the road He has chosen for me. He is in control of opening all the necessary ministry doors along that road.

Within ten months God opened a door for me to start ministering in prisons. I resigned my position with Teen Challenge and rented a small apartment in San Bernardino. I attended Gateway Fellowship Church. Brother Howard Davis was the pastor and wanted me to help with his outreach to the prisons and jails around Southern California.

God then opened yet another door, which turned out to be all the way back across the country, in Reston, Virginia. I started working with Prison Fellowship Ministries in April 1986. Chuck Colson, the well-known aide to former president Richard Nixon, had founded Prison Fellowship ten years earlier. I had gotten to know some of the Prison Fellowship representatives when I was in Lexington. I had attended several of PF's in-prison seminars and Bible studies and was chosen by them to represent my prison at a two-week Washington discipleship program.

PF hired me to go around the United States and set up after-care groups for ex-cons once they got out. We called the program Philemon Fellowship.

I trained leaders in various communities in each state PF had an office, to help care for recently released inmates less than three years after I was released from prison myself. Who says God doesn't have a sense of humor? He knows what each of us needs.

I worked out of PF's offices in Reston for a couple of years. It was great work, helping ex-prisoners connect with local churches and support groups.

But God must have known I needed to go back to the West Coast. After working out of Reston for two years, I moved back to California in 1988, still employed by Prison Fellowship.

One of the things PF wanted me to do in California was offer inmates a weekend Life Action Planning Seminar. We were going to go to the prisons to counsel inmates, talk about their habits and what life would be like once they got out. We provided valuable information for inmates preparing to re-enter society.

Everybody likes the image of going into prisons and "saving" the inmates. But when those inmates leave the protection of the high walls and fences topped with razor wire, they're not always welcomed back into society with open arms.

In those seminars, we looked each inmate in the eye and asked what his needs were. Then we asked, "What do you think it takes to be a successful, well-rounded person?" We offered a simple combination of well-known stress-management practices and Christian teachings, discussing everyday facets of life such as eating right, exercising, and making the right friends. We asked the inmates to think about specific scenarios. For example, "Who will you lean on when you run into trouble after you're out of prison?" and "How will you feel if your first dinner after prison is chips and salsa instead of steak and a baked potato with all the fixings."

This program also sensitized the church to see beyond a prisoner's salvation and look at ways to help fill an inmate's needs once he or she is released from prison. All too many times I found church volunteers only wanted to get prisoners saved and were not trained on what to expect after prison. Many ex-prisoners found wonderful church homes through this fantastic program.

Those things might seem simple, not even worth discussing, but they're important. If they're overlooked, unexpected disappointments can create even bigger problems.

Chapter 17
The B Side

Since my life has always revolved around music—before salvation and prison, anyway—it seemed appropriate to use musical terms to title many of this book's chapters and sections. If you were born after the 1960s, you might not remember the albums mentioned in earlier chapters or those little 45 rpm records. But I do. With a quarter-sized hole in the middle, 45s carried hit singles from those albums—just one. On the flip side of the 45 was a song that might be terrible, or a great find, but never as well known as the A side.

I figured I was entering the B side of my life. I didn't want the fame or fortune of the music business but I finally knew what really mattered. It was knowing I was *now* a child of God, being able to live victoriously *now* as a member of God's spiritual kingdom here on earth, and looking forward to the promise of living *forever* in heaven. Everything else was icing on the cake, especially the peace. There are not enough words in the English language to characterize God's peace. The Bible describes it:

> *And the peace of God, which passeth all understanding, shall keep your hearts and minds through Christ Jesus.* (Philippians 4:7)

In 1989, I had a good life. I rented a home in the San Bernardino Mountains in a town called Running Springs, between Big Bear Lake and Lake Arrowhead. It's one of the most beautiful spots in the world. I was still working for Prison Fellowship, as an area director in Los Angeles. I was managing an all-volunteer staff, delegating responsibilities, serving the Lord. I even won an Outstanding Achievement award from Prison Fellowship.

I couldn't have been happier. Still, I knew that if I ever had the chance, I'd go back to work at Faith Farm. In fact, I mentioned that feeling numerous times to many of my friends.

My phone rang in August 1989. It was Pappy. Why was I not surprised? He had been fasting and praying for two weeks about the direction they should take regarding fill-ing a crucial position: director of evangelism. Pappy said they had received an answer from God and the answer was me. He was sitting with Mike Brown, superintendent of Faith Farm, and they both agreed I was the man for the job.

Talk about a leap of faith! I was very happy in California. I thought I had all I wanted—all the Lord wanted me to have. I was doing His work and feeling like I was doing pretty well at it. Why would I give that up to move all the way back across the country? And yet, I couldn't shake the feeling that I was being called by the Lord. If He had really told Pappy and Mike, as the answer to Pappy's prayer and fasting, that I was God's choice, who was I to say no? I trusted them. I trusted Him. I chose the open door.

My friend Jack "Murph the Surf" Murphy kiddingly advises: "Always go through the doors God opens that are so wide you could drive a freight train through them sideways." This was one of those doors.

I packed everything I owned and moved to Florida.

First, I stopped at the Dunklin Memorial Camp for four months of training. If you or anyone you know ever need help with alcohol or drug abuse, you might want to investigate that place. A wonderful church facility centered in south Florida, Dunklin is nothing like the celebrity world of a Betty Ford Center. It is a spirit-filled ministry that uses biblical principles to help people with substance abuse problems. This approach makes all the difference in the world.

Mickey Evans, who still runs it, founded the camp in 1962. Mickey uses Pappy's no-nonsense type of tough love to help others. The Dunklin program lasts for at least ten months, so it's not easy. But it is effective.

I was there for four months, working with the staff and learning a lot. Dunklin had a tremendous impact on me.

A Farm Foundation

After four months at Dunklin, I traveled to Fort Lauderdale and started work with Faith Farm again, first as director of evangelism there; a few months later, moving to the corporate offices at the Boynton Beach location.

I was on fire. Not because of any wonderful things I did for Faith Farm, but simply because I was faithful in answering God's call.

In 1991 God opened the door for me to go to another ministry. I knew not to try to open my own doors. But if God opened one for me, I needed to step through it.

I prayed about taking the offer, just

as Pappy and Mike had prayed for God to send them someone to do the job of director of evangelism.

It soon became apparent to me that the work God had for me at Faith Farm was done. Rico Lamberti, a friend of mine, wanted me to help him with the work he was doing. It was a new approach to helping people through drug-, alcohol-, and prison-related problems. Rico was a counselor at an organization in Palm Beach County called the Drug Abuse Foundation. The foundation had signed a contract with the Palm Beach County Sheriff's Department to supply drug treatment services for their new program, named the Drug Farm. It was a boot camp, the second of its kind in the US. I was offered a job as court liaison.

Think about it: an ex-con, who had served time on a drug conviction, standing up in court at a sentencing hearing to speak up for someone else who had been convicted on drug charges. Sound ridiculous? It wasn't. In fact, that was exactly what God led me to do.

Still, I had my doubts. Before I started the job, I thought, *Who am I to stand up in court to say this guy has changed and that he won't do it again?*

But I knew the Lord can fix that sort of situation. He uses people who are shy and uncomfortable just like He uses people who

are bold and self-assured. He can use anyone
. . . anyone who allows Him to, that is.

So there I was in 1991, seven years
after my release from prison, going to court
in Palm Beach County, Florida, to help convicted criminals. I was doing for them what
Detective Rossi had done for me a decade
earlier. Sometimes the ways God works
aren't so mysterious.

I spent most of my time meeting with
lawyers and judges, discussing the many
cases in court each day. I explained to them
how the program worked, what was
involved. Most prosecutors and defense attorneys, along with the judges, were in favor of
sending inmates to the Drug Farm. They all
liked it because they saw many people go
through their courts with drug problems and
they had no programs to send them to. The
judges and attorneys had seen the revolving
door of people coming through the court system with a drug conviction, incarceration,
release, and then a return conviction . . . the
same people running through the system year
after year.

The Drug Farm was designed to be a
minimum-security program for first-time
offenders. Participants had to stay at the farm
for a year and then go through three years of
probation. So a prison sentence of lesser
length looked like a better deal to some peo-

ple.

But that would be their loss. The Drug Farm was, and still is, an extremely successful program. The combination of hard work and teaching of Christian values has worked time and time again. An independent study recently showed almost 90 percent of the inmates who completed the program have stayed clean and were never re-arrested. That's phenomenal.

Being part of the program did me a lot of good too. I'm not sure why, but I became a big hit around the courthouse. All the judges wanted to know how the program was doing and were thrilled to hear the people they sentenced to it were being changed. I really felt I was involved in a very important life-saving project.

The Emergence of Understanding

My work with the Drug Abuse Foundation was professionally fulfilling. I was thrilled to be a part of this great organization. I stayed with DAF for five years working as the sheriff's Drug Farm's court liaison and later as Supervisor of Information Services, Medical Records, and Case Management.

In 1995 my father, who was eighty-two, developed Parkinson's disease and desperately needed my help. So I took a leave of absence and left the Drug Abuse Foundation and moved to Fort Lauderdale. I saw this as another ministry in which God wanted me to serve Him.

During the next two years, my father and I grew a little closer. It took a lot of work because he was a rather cool, distant person. But I was glad for the progress we made.

He passed away in 1997, leaving me to care for my mom. I remained loyal to her and to my ministry, but I still had choices to make in my life. I've learned, sometimes the hard way; to make choices based on the will of God. I still have plenty to work on. But I do understand that:

> ***The fruit of the Spirit is love, joy, peace, longsuffering, gentleness, goodness, faith, meekness, temperance.*** **(Galatians 5:22-23)**

The Next-to-Last Act

This book has been a labor of love. I started writing it by hand in 1983, while I was in prison. I had wanted to write a testimony book ever since I read Frank Costantino's *Holes in Time*. That book had a profound impact on me. I had never heard the gospel from someone who'd been in trouble—only from priests and ministers. I didn't know "bad guys" could ever become "good

200

guys." I learned this by reading Frank's book. He claimed he was one of the worst, yet God saved him and made him a new creature in Christ Jesus. I wanted that. And I hope to convey that same feeling to anyone who reads this book.

I wrote most of this book while I was in prison, and I wrote about my life up to that point. After I got out, I let it sit, not paying much attention to it or thinking about what I would do with it if I ever finished it. I did write a short version of my testimony, which appeared in the January 1987 issue of *Voice* magazine. That opened doors for me to appear with Pat Robertson on the *700 Club* television show and have my story dramatized on the *Unshackled* radio program.

After several years I revisited the notion of getting my story published. In 1995, Chaplain Ray Hoekstra—known in ministry and prison circles as Chaplain Ray, now deceased—wanted me to finish the book so he could publish it for use in his work. But I wasn't available to travel to speak in prisons and churches to support it because of my obligation to my mother. So I put the book on hold again. It wasn't time to go through that door . . . not yet.

I went back to work on the book in 2002. Working on it through the following year, while still caring for my mother, I learned a lot. I thought it would take less time than it did. But different problems came and went, and work on the book was slow. (Slow in our time—I often need to remind myself that God's work is done in His time.) While I was caring for my mother, I couldn't do much work on the book. After 2004, when Mom passed away, I renewed my commitment to finish the work. Another door was opening. It was time.

Timing is everything. This book is part of God's plan. He knew you would hold it in your hands, that your eyes would see these words and that my story would reach you.

He also knows that you have decisions to make. If you have not yet received Jesus Christ as your Lord and Savior, you have that choice to make first.

The time is now. Don't wait.

If you'd like, you could say this simple prayer right now to ask Jesus to come into your life:

> Jesus, I know that I have broken
> Your laws and my sins have separated me from You. I am truly sorry,
> and now I want to turn away from
> my past sinful life towards You.
> Please forgive me, and help me avoid
> sinning again. I believe that You died
> for my sins, were resurrected from

the dead, are alive, and hear my prayer. I invite You to become the Lord and Savior of my life, to rule and reign in my heart from this day forward. Please baptize me with Your Holy Spirit to help me obey You, and to do Your will for the rest of my life. It is in Your name that I pray, Jesus.   Amen.

After you have accepted Jesus Christ, your own experiences will become your unique testimony. I have discovered, and continue to find, that my life matters. Your life matters too. If my story has helped you, I encourage you to tell your story to others. God may not be calling you to write a book. He might want you to just talk to the people around you, your friends, family, and coworkers. Or He could be opening doors for you to become involved in a ministry, either part time or full time, to help others.

Be open to His leading. Watch for the doors He opens for you. Then walk through them, confident that the One who is always with you will always be with you, every step of life's journey.

Cadet Marty Angelo at Cardinal Farley
Military Academy, 1963

Marty Angelo and his blues band, 1966

Marty Angelo with Raven band members at the
infamous Steve Paul's Scene, 1968

Marty Angelo rock 'n' roll
band manager, 1969

Marty Angelo
bar owner, 1970

Marty Angelo and Eddie Rivera, founder of
International Disco Record Centre, 1976

Marty Angelo "on the set" with the *Disco Step-
by-Step*® dancers, 1976

Marty Angelo receives Prison Fellowship's
Outstanding Service Award, June 1989
Charles W. Colson (founder, Prison Fellowship
Ministries), Marty Angelo, governor Albert H.
Quie (former governor of Minnesota and former
president of Prison Fellowship Ministries)

Ron Sharp, Mel Goebel, Marty Angelo, 1989

Disco Step-by-Step® producer Marty Angelo
and director Paul C. Hanson, 1978

Marty Angelo and the late Rev. Garland "Pappy"
Eastham (founder, Faith Farm Ministries), 1985

Mickey Evans (founder, Dunklin Memorial Camp)
and Marty Angelo, 1987

Jack "Murph the Surf" Murphy, Bob Erler, Frank
Costantino, Marty Angelo, Mark Marciel, 1988